Exploring Canada

ONTARIO

Titles in the Exploring Canada series include:

Alberta

British Columbia

Manitoba

Quebec

Yukon Territory

Exploring Canada

ONTARIO

by Steven Ferry

LUCENT
BOOKS®

THOMSON
™
GALE

San Diego • Detroit • New York • San Francisco • Cleveland • New Haven, Conn. • Waterville, Maine • London • Munich

Development, management, design, and composition by Pre-Press Company, Inc.

LIBRARY OF CONGRESS CATALOGING-IN-PUBLICATION DATA

Ferry, Steven. 1953–
  Ontario / by Steven Ferry.
      p. cm. — (Exploring Canada series)
  Summary: Examines the history, geography, climate, industries, people and culture of
what is by far the most populous of Canada's provinces.
  Includes bibliographical references and index.
    ISBN 1-59018-050-X (lib. bdg. : alk. paper)
   1. Ontario—Juvenile literature. [1. Ontario 2. Canada.] I. Title. II. Series.
F1057.4 .F47 2003
971.3—dc21

                                                                          2002014351

Printed in the United States of America

Contents

Foreword

A ny truly accurate portrait of Canada would have to be painted in sharp contrasts, for this is a long-inhabited but only recently settled land. It is a vast and expansive region peopled by a predominantly urban population. Canada is also a nation of natives and immigrants that, as its Prime Minister Lester Pearson remarked in the late 1960s, has "not yet found a Canadian soul except in time of war." Perhaps it is in these very contrasts that this elusive national identity is waiting to be found.

Canada as an inhabited place is among the oldest in the Western Hemisphere, having accepted prehistoric migrants more than eleven thousand years ago after they crossed a land bridge where the Bering Strait now separates Alaska from Siberia. Canada is also the site of the New World's earliest European settlement, L'Anse aux Meadows on the northern tip of Newfoundland Island. A band of Vikings lived there briefly some five hundred years before Columbus reached the West Indies in 1492.

Yet as a nation Canada is still a relative youngster on the world scene. It gained its independence almost a century after the American Revolution and half a century after the wave of nationalist uprisings in South America. Canada did not include Newfoundland until 1949 and could not amend its own constitution without approval from the British Parliament until 1982. "The Sleeping Giant," as Canada is sometimes known, came within a whisker of losing a province in 1995, when the people of Quebec narrowly voted down an independence referendum. In 1999 Canada carved out a new territory, Nunavut, which has a population equal to that of Key West, Florida, spread over an area the size of Alaska and California combined.

As the second largest country in the world (after Russia), the land itself is also famously diverse. British Columbia's "Pocket Desert" near the town of Osoyoos is the northernmost desert in North America. A few hundred miles away, in Alberta's Banff National Park, one can walk on the Columbia Icefields, the largest nonpolar icecap in the world. In parts of Manitoba and the Yukon glacially created sand dunes creep slowly across the landscape. Quebec and Ontario have so many lakes in the boundless north that tens of thousands remain unnamed.

One can only marvel at a place where the contrasts range from the profound (the first medical use of insulin) to the mundane (the invention of Trivial Pursuit); the sublime (the poetry of Ontario-born Robertson Davies) to the ridiculous (the comic antics of Ontario-born Jim Carrey); the British (ever-so-quaint Victoria) to the French (Montreal, the world's second-largest French-speaking city); and the environmental (Greenpeace was founded in Vancouver) to the industrial (refuse from nickel mining near Sudbury, Ontario left a landscape so barren that American astronauts used it to train for their moon walks).

Given these contrasts and conflicts, can this national experiment known as Canada survive? Or to put it another way, what is it that unites as Canadians the elderly Inuit woman selling native crafts in the Yukon; the millionaire businessman-turned-restaurateur recently emigrated from Hong Kong to Vancouver; the mixed-French (Métis) teenager living in a rural settlement in Manitoba; the cosmopolitan French-speaking professor of archaeology in Quebec City; and the raw-boned Nova Scotia fisherman struggling to make a living? These are questions only Canadians can answer, and perhaps will have to face for many decades.

A true portrait of Canada can't, therefore, be provided by a brief essay, any more than a snapshot captures the entire life of a centenarian. But the Exploring Canada series can offer an illuminating overview of individual provinces and territories. Each book smartly summarizes an area's geography, history, arts and culture, daily life, and contemporary issues. Read individually or as a series, they show that what Canadians undeniably have in common is a shared heritage as people who came, whether in past millennia or last year, to a land with a difficult climate and a challenging geography, yet somehow survived and worked with one another to form a vibrant whole.

Land of People and Water

The name Ontario was first applied to Lake Ontario in 1641 and is traceable to Native North American sources. It may be a corruption of the Iroquoian word *Onitariio*, meaning "beautiful lake," or *Kanadario*, variously translated as "sparkling" or "beautiful" water. Later European settlers gave the name to the land along the lakeshore and then to an ever-extending area around it. Nineteenth-century historian Henry Scadding suggested that Ontario might have come from the Seneca *Entouhonorous*, meaning "the people"—the name that the Seneca Indians used for themselves.

Whether Ontario refers to the people or the water, today it has plenty of both. The province's population of 11.4 million represents one-third of Canada's total population. The Toronto metropolitan area holds some 4.7 million people, making it the largest metropolitan area in Canada. Although Ontario is by far the most populated province in Canada, much of its vast land is still wild and rugged, as if reminding its inhabitants that they are there only for a few millennia before the next great ice sheet comes grinding down from the north. It is a province that is defined by its bordering bodies of water: the St. Lawrence River, four of the five Great Lakes (all but Lake Michigan border Ontario), Lake Huron's enormous Georgian Bay (which is almost as big as Lake Ontario), the Hudson Bay and its James Bay. Rivers and lakes account for more than one-sixth of Ontario's territory, and this abundance of freshwater played a major role in the province's history.

Beyond "Old Ontario"

■ *One-sixth of Ontario's territory is made up of lakes and rivers.*

The original inhabitants of Ontario came from the west. They were hunter-gatherers from Asia who traveled into North America via the Bering Strait land bridge during the last Ice Age. Later people arrived from the east—French and English explorers, traders, and settlers. They came looking for fur, trade routes to China, or just a better life. Many of Ontario's subsequent immigrants were simply fleeing something, whether the American War of Independence, the Irish potato famine, or Cambodian political upheaval.

Originally, almost all the newcomers to present-day Canada settled in the narrow band of land around the St. Lawrence River and the Great Lakes. "Old Ontario," a term sometimes loosely applied to the southern portion of the province, is where the combination of rich soil and moderate climate is most suitable for supporting an agrarian lifestyle. The land held immense riches beyond Old Ontario, though. Farther west, grain crops like wheat could thrive on the plains. Throughout the deciduous forests of the south and the coniferous forests to the north, seemingly limitless numbers of trees could provide lumber. In the extensive and inhospitable Canadian Shield area that sweeps around the Hudson Bay, minerals were abundant. Power was available from the tens of thousands of rivers and lakes in Ontario and beyond. It was the people of old Canada, including Ontario, who first opened up and peopled these previously unexplored and mostly uninhabited lands.

For most of Ontario's early history, it was ruled by the British. Their influence left an unmistakable mark on the province. However diverse Ontario's ethnic groups are today, nothing can eradicate the area's British heritage. In Toronto's hinterland, town names are mostly British, such as Durham, Exeter, Newmarket, Waterloo, Cambridge, and London (inevitably located on the river Thames). There is even a town called Stratford, which holds an annual Shakespeare Festival.

But Ontario is also home to other people, such as the French who founded towns with names like Fauquier, Plantagenet, and St. Eugène, and the Germans who founded towns they called Berlin, New Prussia, and New Hamburg. While carving out an existence for themselves and their families, the people of Ontario, whether their heritage is Native Canadian ("First Nations"), British, French, German, African, or Asian, have had to accept the extreme geographical and climatic features of the land they inhabited: the barren tundra of the far north, the piercingly cold winters, the storms that sweep over the land from the lakes. Nature at its rawest is beyond human control yet the people of Ontario have coerced remarkable accommodations from nature, including the St. Lawrence Seaway, hydroelectric power from plants on the Niagara and many other rivers, and the mazelike underground city in downtown Toronto, Ontario's capital.

"Doing Quite Nicely, Thank You"

Home to one out of every eight Canadians, Toronto serves as the preeminent center of Canadian business, finance, culture, fashion, publishing, and communication. Ontario's second-largest city, Ottawa, is Canada's capital and home to the Canadian federal government. The province itself has become a major global player, too, exporting billions of dollars worth of autos, metals, machines, and other goods each year to its southern neighbor, the United States, as well as to countries around the world.

Over the centuries since the Europeans first encountered Native Canadians on the Atlantic coast, Canadians have created a transcontinental nation of many peoples. Ontario has always played a prominent role in this development. Today, whatever

■ *The sun sets above the majestic Toronto skyline and the shimmering water of Lake Ontario.*

one's interests, Ontario can fulfill them with its diverse resources and cultural activities. It has deservedly earned the reputation of providing one of the highest standards of living in the world.

An editorial in the *Toronto Globe and Mail* in the mid-1980s stated it quite succinctly: "We are a long way from realizing our full potential, but still doing quite nicely, thank you, in comparison with most other nations in the world, whether we measure by bellies filled or freedoms enjoyed."[1]

Learning to live together remains a challenge for all Canadians. The challenge for the people of Ontario will be to maintain the balance they have achieved in their multicultural society and continue to create those high standards of living for everyone, especially in the face of the rapidly changing global backdrop of the twenty-first century.

From Tundra to Toronto

T he second-largest Canadian province, behind only Quebec, Ontario is located in the east-central part of Canada and encompasses roughly one-tenth of Canada's overall size. On the south, Ontario borders the United States, separated by Lake Superior, Lake Huron, Lake Erie, Lake Ontario, and the southernmost section of the St. Lawrence River. Defining Ontario's northern borders are the mighty James and Hudson Bays, bodies of water that Ontario shares with its neighbor Quebec to the east. Geographically, Ontario is divided into three major regions: the stark Hudson Bay lowlands to the north and northwest, the vast forests of the Canadian Shield in the middle of the province, and the fertile St. Lawrence lowlands in the very south.

The Frozen North

The Hudson Bay lowlands extend approximately 100 to 200 miles (160 to 320 kilometers) inland from the shores of Ontario's James Bay and Hudson Bay. In total the Hudson Bay lowlands make up a huge infertile plain about the size of the state of Arizona. Continuous permafrost (permanently frozen subsoil) and the potential for freezing weather year-round make this an inhospitable area for humans. The few small towns in this area are populated mostly by First Nations people and are located where major rivers like the Moose and the Albany spill into the James Bay. Outside of these small towns no roads penetrate the Hudson Bay lowlands.

Canada's Capitals and Major Cities

GREENLAND

UNITED STATES

- ⊕ National capital
- ★ Provincial or territorial capitals
- · Major cities

YUKON TERRITORY

BAFFIN ISLAND

NORTHWEST TERRITORIES

Yellowknife

NUNAVUT

Labrador Sea

BRITISH COLUMBIA

Pacific Ocean

ALBERTA

Hudson Bay

QUEBEC

NEWFOUNDLAND

Edmonton ★

SASKATCHEWAN

MANITOBA

St. John's

Vancouver

·Calgary

ONTARIO

Winnipeg

UNITED STATES

NOVA SCOTIA

Montreal

Halifax

Ottawa ⊛

NEW BRUNSWICK

Toronto

Atlantic Ocean

A thin strip of the northernmost Hudson Bay lowlands, including much of Polar Bear Provincial Park, is covered by tundra. Barren and treeless, tundra supports only the hardiest plant life—mostly low-lying bushes, grasses, sedges (tufted marsh plants), and mosses and lichens. Animals include not only polar bears but also arctic fox, snow geese, and caribou. Beyond the coastal tundra, innumerable rivers, peat bogs, and shallow lakes and ponds characterize the marshy landscape.

Slightly farther south, the permafrost becomes discontinuous and a transition forest features sporadic stands of tamarack, spruce, and other trees. Few of these trees, however, attain a height of more than forty feet (twelve meters) or so. Alder and willow form the undergrowth; sphagnum, feather, and other mosses can also be found. Sedges, grasses, and shrubs like Labrador tea form the ground vegetation, interspersed by hummocks and peat plateaus that rise to twenty feet (six meters) in height. It is estimated that peat accumulates from decayed sphagnum moss and aquatic plants and grasses at a rate of about an inch every twenty years.

The Canadian Shield

Directly to the south of this transition forest lies an area that is peculiarly Canadian: the broad and ancient battlefield of glaciers known as the Canadian Shield. The Shield is a massive, geologically stable, structural unit of the earth's crust that stretches over much of eastern and central Canada. It covers a large part of Ontario, with the exception of the Hudson Bay lowlands to the north and the fertile regions of the Great Lakes and the St. Lawrence River in the south. Its Precambrian rock is among the oldest existing geographical features in the world, and surface rocks have been dated back 600 million years. The landscape of the Shield is dramatic, with its rock outcrops, coniferous forests, marshland, and lakes and rivers.

The ancient Shield area of Ontario is rich in minerals, such as iron, copper, zinc, silver, and nickel. Much of it is also heavily forested. These Shield resources exist, however, in a climate and environment that are generally hostile to human habitation. Because of this, it takes resourceful individuals to survive there. As Jay and Audrey Walz note in *Portrait of Canada*:

> [The Canadian Shield] is strewn with lakes, 250,000 of them in its Ontario sector alone, much of it is beautiful and, to the north, rich in ores. As farmland the thinly covered ancient stone broke the hearts of most of the pioneers who ventured this far. In central Ontario descendants of those who hung on live in hard poverty where they try to farm rocky soil. Others have given up; and abandoned farms, their barns and sheds fallen in, mark the roadside for many a mile. Around the next bend, however, the motorist may be surprised to see prosperous rolling farmland, usually lying in a wide river valley.[2]

Although not as sparsely populated as the Hudson Bay lowlands, much of the area of the Canadian Shield in Ontario is still wilderness. In addition to the occasional mineral extraction site, numerous Indian reserves are located on remote Shield lakes. Most of these native settlements are

■ How Glaciers Shaped the Land

Glaciers have shaped almost all of Canada's geography. Ice sheets have re-
peatedly covered some 97 percent of the Canadian surface over the last 2
million years. The advancing and retreating sheets of ice, often up to two
miles (three kilometers) thick, relentlessly pushed their way across the
land that is now Canada and into the northern parts of the United States.
Just eighteen thousand years ago, an ice sheet as large as Antarctica covered much of present-day Ontario. Upon melting and retreating, these ice
sheets left many clues to their presence, including deep scratches on surface rock, piles of pushed up or deposited soil and rock (moraines), and
scattered boulders (erratics). The ice sheets were so heavy that the land is
still rebounding from the removal of the weight of the last glacier, which
retreated about ten thousand years ago. Parts of the Hudson Bay lowlands,
in fact, are rising at a rate of fifty inches per century, the continent's highest rate of uplift.

Eons of rain, snow, and moving ice have exposed and eroded parts of
the Canadian Shield in central Ontario—the Shield is not as resistant as its
name implies. When rock meets water, over time the water always wins.
Where the hard rock of the Shield has been scraped clean of its soil by
glaciers, the resulting drainage patterns create the familiar marshes, bogs,
shallow lakes, and meandering rivers. Runoff from the melting of the most

not served by any roads and can be reached only by small
aircraft.

From Forests to Lowlands

The central and northwestern parts of Ontario are covered by
boreal (northern) forest, sometimes referred to as taiga. Although there may be isolated patches of permafrost in the
northern areas, the land is completely free of permafrost in
the southern regions. Ontario's boreal forest is part of the
global taiga that encircles the Northern Hemisphere, making
up the single largest ecosystem on the earth and accounting
for one-third of the world's total forests. In all, the world's boreal forests cover almost 6 million square miles (15 million
square kilometers) in Canada, Alaska, Russia, Scandinavia,
and Asia. This ancient forest of spruce, fir, larch, hemlock, and
pine extends across Canada in a huge swath that runs all the
way from the east coast to the Rockies, an area that represents
roughly one-quarter of the world's taiga. Ontario's boreal for-

recent massive ice sheet also helped to create the huge lakes and river systems around the perimeter of the shield—from the inland seas in the far north of Canada such as Great Bear Lake, Great Slave Lake, and Lake Athabasca, to Lake Winnipeg in Manitoba, Ontario's Lake of the Woods, the five Great Lakes, and the St. Lawrence River system.

As a result of the glaciers' onslaught and the short growing season of the far north, the vast majority of Ontario's landmass is difficult to farm. Much of this land is rich in natural resources, however, including lumber, minerals, and hydroelectric potential.

■ *Fissures known as crevasses give this glacier a rugged and weathered appearance. The movement of glaciers shaped much of Ontario's topography.*

est is thick and trackless, dotted with innumerable lakes, rivers, and swamps. The soil is generally poor but many kinds of wildlife thrive in environments untouched by humans.

Ontario's populated lowlands are enclosed in a roughly triangular area that is approximately 400 miles (650 kilometers) on each side. The three points of the triangle can be defined by Sault Sainte Marie, at the junction of Lake Superior and Lake Huron, in the west; Ottawa in the east; and Windsor, at the junction of Lake Huron and Lake Erie, in the south. Sometimes referred to as the Great Lakes–St. Lawrence lowlands, this corner of Ontario comprises only about 10 percent of Ontario's land. It houses, however, the bulk of the province's population and its major urban centers.

Along with the cities, suburbs, and farmlands, plenty of forest remains even in this populated section of Ontario. Being a transition zone between coniferous and deciduous forests, southern Ontario has some of both. South of the Ottawa River, and in the area of the huge Algonquin Provincial Park, beech and maple forests dominate while white oak, hickory, walnut, basswood, and black cherry can also be seen. The natural tree cover in the Great Lakes–St. Lawrence lowlands has been good not only for clearing the land for farming, but also for harvesting the evergreens such as spruce and highly valuable white pine.

A Climate of Extremes

Ontario's climate varies considerably from the north, influenced by arctic air masses, to the south, where the Great Lakes have a moderating effect. The provincial climate also changes dramatically from season to season. Here's how a recent government study summarized Ontario's climate:

> In Northern Ontario, the climate is primarily continental, with cold winters and mild summers. Most precipitation falls in the form of summer showers and thunderstorms; winter snowfall amounts can be impressive, but usually contain less water. . . . The combination of uniform precipitation amounts year-round, delayed spring and autumn, and moderated temperatures in winter and summer makes

■ *Ontario's snow-filled winters make ice-skating a popular pastime.*

■ Uncommon Hazards

Ontario is far from the earthquake-prone Pacific "rim of fire," as well as the "tornado alley" in the American Midwest. Yet the province has experienced its share of natural disasters, including both earthquakes and tornadoes. Most memorably, in September 1944 at Cornwall, east of Ottawa on the St. Lawrence, an earthquake that registered 6.4 on the Richter scale caused an estimated $1 million worth of damage. The spate of tornadoes that hit the area of Sarnia, at the southern tip of Lake Huron, in May 1953 left five people dead.

The more common types of natural disasters in Ontario include lengthy droughts and fierce storms—those on the Great Lakes can generate huge, ship-sinking waves. The droughts that affected Ontario in 1949 and again in 1955, for example, each caused upwards of $100 million of damage. In 1954, Hurricane Hazel hit the province, causing about one hundred deaths and $2 million in damage. The devastating ice storm that struck Quebec and Ontario in January 1998 was Canada's first $1 billion insurance loss.

Ontario also once experienced an especially deadly lightning storm. It occurred on July 29, 1916, when lightning ignited a forest fire that burned down the towns of Cochrane and Matheson, 170 miles (275 kilometers) north of Sudbury, killing 233 people.

Southern Ontario's climate one of the most suitable in Canada for both agriculture and human settlement.[3]

Although Toronto lies roughly on the same latitude as the French Riviera, the city typically experiences a winter in which the average daily low temperature is below freezing for five months of the year (November through March). Toronto also has its share of beautiful weather—average daily highs from May to September range from 65° to 79° F (18° to 26° C), not much different from the weather in southern New England. This part of Canada is milder than most outsiders realize—a popular apocryphal story of Toronto locals tells of Americans who get off the plane in Toronto during July carrying their skis.

Winters can vary widely not only from north to south but also from year to year. In winter 2000–2001, southern Ontario endured 104 consecutive days of snow cover. The following year snow was scarce in southern Ontario and there were no nighttime lows below 5° F (−15° C) compared to an average year of twenty such lows.

■ *The arboreal, mask-faced raccoon is just one of Ontario's many mammal species.*

Because of the southern location and the influence of the Great Lakes, the climate on the so-called Ontario Peninsula (the land situated between Lake Erie, Lake Huron, and Georgian Bay) is Canada's most temperate. With its fertile soil and relatively long growing season, this makes the peninsula by far the province's most favorable area for farming. Among the crops grown are corn, carrots, and lettuce. Livestock such as dairy cattle and hogs are also raised here. The Ontario Peninsula supports large orchards of apples, cherries, pears, plums, and even peaches. Local variations also create microclimates that are useful for growing specialized crops such as wine grapes.

Abundant and Diverse Wildlife

The abundant plant diversity in central and southern Ontario supports a wide variety of mammals, amphibians, and birds. Biologists have identified hundreds of different types of mammals in Ontario, including deer, moose, caribou, coyotes, wolves, foxes (gray, red, and arctic), mountain lions and bobcats, black and polar bears, raccoons, weasels, mink, and wolverines. Smaller animals include dozens of rodents, such as porcupines, muskrats, lemmings, beaver, flying squirrels, chipmunks, and woodchucks. In the winter of 1998, wildlife officials released into the northern Ontario forest fifty wapiti taken from Alberta. A large species of deer also known as American elk, the animals were common in Ontario until overhunting and habitat destruction eliminated them around 1900.

Ontario's numerous lakes, rivers, and wetlands are a largely undisturbed haven for hundreds of species of ducks, herons, sandpipers, and other birds, including those that remain in the province year round and those that migrate farther south every summer. Ontario's waters are also home to many species of fish, including warm-water species such as carp, white perch, and largemouth bass, and cold-water species such as rainbow trout, chinook salmon, and lake sturgeon. Fishing, a way of life for Ontario's earliest inhabitants, remains a viable commercial enterprise as well as a popular recreational pastime for modern Canadians.

Ontario's Great Lakes

More so than anywhere else in Canada, water is an important feature of Ontario's landscape. Of the province's almost unimaginable quarter of a million lakes, some thirty-nine hundred are larger than one square mile (three square kilometers) in size. The largest, of course, are the Great Lakes, which are more like freshwater inland seas. They contain about fifty-five hundred cubic miles (twenty-three thousand cubic kilometers) of water, and cover a total area about the size of the state of Wyoming. Taken together they make up the largest system of fresh surface water on earth, representing roughly 18 percent of the world's freshwater supply. Only the polar ice caps contain more freshwater.

Ontario also has many rivers, including the mighty St. Lawrence. Once called "Canada's Highway," the St. Lawrence River drains the Great Lakes basin into the Atlantic Ocean. The St. Lawrence is young compared with other rivers—perhaps only a few thousand years old in its current location. Because large ships could not easily navigate parts of it, a joint Canadian/American project in the 1950s led to the 1959 opening of the St. Lawrence Seaway. The series of canals and locks built from Lake Superior to Montreal permanently connected the heart of Canada to the Atlantic Ocean. When sections of the seaway—even saltwater sections—freeze over between December and April, a dozen icebreakers keep lanes

■ Taming the Thunder of Water

The Neutral Indians who lived in southern Ontario used gestures and an unusual Iroquoian dialect to explain to the first Europeans that there was a place where the river falls from a rock higher than the tallest pines, causing a "thunder of water." Based on the sound of the word, the Europeans wrote down *Onguiaahra*. Many years and numerous misspellings later, the name evolved as Niagara. It may well represent the only word left behind by the Neutral, who were basically wiped out as a people by 1650 due to the effects of smallpox and intertribal warfare.

Although the Neutral and other native tribes no doubt regarded the falls with awe, the falls also posed a practical problem, since they were obviously impassable in birch-bark canoes. Instead, the Indians had to scale the riverbanks and portage around the falls. In 1678, a party under the command of the French explorer René-Robert La Salle sailed a large ship up the Niagara River to a series of rapids just above the falls. The French persuaded the Indians to show them their portage route. The French then carried six tons of supplies and seven dismantled cannons ten miles, and built another ship, the *Griffon*, beyond the falls. The *Griffon* was the first ship ever to enter Lake Erie.

The British later built the first railway on the North American continent right up the face of the steep slope to carry goods from arriving ships, thus doing away with the need to portage goods.

open to traffic. Today enormous grain and ore carriers navigate the Great Lakes all the way to Thunder Bay, Ontario, on the western shore of Lake Superior. Thunder Bay's busy port facilities transfer goods to and from rail freight cars, trucks, and ships, allowing Canadian products to reach markets across the country and around the world.

Rivers and Falls

A major feature of southeastern Ontario is the Niagara Escarpment, a steep rock face that runs some 450 miles (725 kilometers) in length, from Niagara, past the southern tip of Lake Ontario, and on to Manitoulin Island, off the end of the Bruce Peninsula that juts into Lake Huron. The escarpment reaches a height of more than 1,100 feet (335 meters) in places, though its most famous site, Niagara Falls, is one-fifth that height. The escarpment was formed by the retreat of the

■ *An aerial view of Niagara Falls dramatically captures the volume and sheer force of the water that plummets from the Niagara Escarpment.*

last continental ice sheet ten thousand to twelve thousand years ago and by the effects of water erosion on the shore of an ancient sea that once covered much of present-day Michigan and parts of southern Ontario.

The waters of Lake Erie and the other Great Lakes flow into Lake Ontario through the 36-mile (58-kilometer) -long Niagara River and its famous falls, which are the world's greatest by water volume. Niagara Falls is actually two falls. The American Falls at 210 feet (64 meters) is about 33 feet (10 meters) higher than the Canadian, or Horseshoe, Falls. The latter, however, at 2,215 feet (675 meters) wide, is more than twice the length and has a flow that is about ten times the volume of the American Falls. As in colonial times, when sawmills and gristmills were built on the banks of the Niagara River to harness its energy, power stations both above and below the falls today supply energy to surrounding towns and cities in Ontario and New York.

The Ottawa River, the largest tributary of the St. Lawrence, runs along Ontario's border with Quebec. For many years, the Ottawa served as a route into the interior for explorers, fur traders, and missionaries. Today, the abundant rapids and its convenient location close to major urban centers make it a very popular recreational river.

An Urban People in a Rural Place

Much like the early pioneers and before them the tribes of the First Nations, most of Ontario's current population is concentrated within the Great Lakes–St. Lawrence lowlands. Ontario's predominantly urban and suburban population reflects a trend within Canada away from a rural, farm-based life and toward an increasingly postindustrial economy.

From the time the earliest peoples claimed the land from the retreating glaciers, those who have chosen to live in present-day Ontario have found ways to survive the challenges posed by nature. The many new waves of people who came to live off the land also found plenty of challenges in learning to interact with and live with each other.

The Natives and the Fur Traders

Ontario's earliest inhabitants are believed to have been descendants of people who came from the Asian mainland. The first such arrivals are thought to have made it to parts of present-day Ontario approximately ten thousand years ago. It was not until perhaps 5000 B.C., however, that First Nations cultures began to take on the distinctive forms—basically northern woodland and southern lowlands—that were noted on the arrival of the first Europeans four centuries ago.

The Woodland Nations

When Henry Hudson was making his fateful final voyage into the Hudson Bay and James Bay in 1610–1611, the native population between these bays and the Great Lakes consisted of the Woodland Nations of the northern forests and the Great Lakes Nations of the Great Lakes–St. Lawrence lowlands. The Woodland Nations consisted of eight principal tribes, all of which spoke languages belonging to the Algonquian family. In present-day Ontario, the Ojibwa (also known as Chippewa) occupied a large territory encompassing the northern shores of Lake Huron and Lake Superior from the Georgian Bay to the edge of the prairies. The Algonquin lived in the Ottawa Valley and the Ottawa lived mainly on Manitoulin Island in the northern Lake Huron, Georgian Bay area.

North and west of the Ojibwa, the Cree occupied an immense area on the southern perimeter of Hudson Bay, as far north as present-day Churchill, Manitoba. Their territory was bounded on the east by Lake Mistassini in Quebec, and extended all the way west to the prairie frontier. It included all of the north and northwestern areas of present-day Ontario.

The Great Lakes Nations

The Great Lakes Nations were divided into nine principal Iroquoian tribes. All of them spoke languages belonging to the Iroquoian family. Within Ontario, the Huron lived between Lake Simcoe and Georgian Bay. To the south and west were their allies, the Tobacco Nation (also called the Petun). Farther south still, on the Niagara Peninsula, lived the Neutral. (The French explorer Samuel de Champlain misnamed this tribe in 1615—they were as apt as other tribes to form alliances and participate in local wars.) The Algonquin Nations mainly survived by hunting and gathering, whereas the Iroquois Nations had developed agriculture and subsisted almost entirely off the fruits of their agricultural labor.

Like their Algonquin neighbors, the Iroquois Nations spoke a number of different dialects. But unlike the Algonquin, they had formed several separate and often mutually hostile nations. The first of these was the Iroquois Confederacy or Five Nations. This alliance consisted of the Mohawk, Oneida, Onondaga, Cayuga, and Seneca. In 1722, they were joined by a sixth tribe, the Tuscarora. The confederacy nations mainly lived south of Lake Ontario in an area that extended to the upper St. Lawrence River. In self-defense, the Huron

■ *A bronze statue of a Huron scout overlooks the Ottawa River and the capital city's Parliament Hill. The Huron ultimately teamed up with the Tobacco, the Neutral, and the Erie tribes to form the Huron Nation.*

had teamed up with the Tobacco, the Neutral, and the Erie to create the Huron Nation.

The Huron and Iroquois confederacies were fairly evenly matched and the hostilities between them might have continued indefinitely if not for the arrival of the well-armed Europeans. Early European explorers did not realize they had walked into the middle of ongoing hostilities and that by taking sides (as the French did with the Algonquin and Huron against the Five Nations), they might incur the wrath of the opposition. In the long run, thousands of people, both Europeans and natives, paid for this mistake with their lives.

Seminomadic Forest Dwellers

Northern woodland tribes, such as the Algonquin, Ojibwa, Ottawa, and Cree, survived by hunting and gathering food off the land. For them, daily life was dictated by the season. In winter, most tribes hunted deer, caribou, and moose. In spring and summer they ate fish, seal, beaver, and the flesh and eggs of birds. They gathered shellfish, roots, and berries, drying and storing the surplus for periods of shortage. In the fall they returned to hunting.

These tribes had perfected a seminomadic way of life suited for hunters in the great forested region that stretched from what is now Nova Scotia into Manitoba. For the often-rough waterways and portages where boats must be carried, they had developed a light birch-bark canoe. The Algonquin made good use of these canoes, notes First Nations historian Lee Sultzman, "to travel great distances for trade, and their strategic location on the Ottawa River became the preferred route between the French on the St. Lawrence River and the tribes of the western Great Lakes."[4] For winter travel they had invented the toboggan and the snowshoe. Because they were constantly moving around in search of game, Algonquin and other northern woodland tribes lived in conical birch-bark tepees or domed wigwams, which they could quickly set up and break down.

They made good use of materials provided by nature and taught woodland skills to the first French explorers. For example, the Woodland Nations used clay, wood, and bark to make cooking utensils and dishes, while birch bark was used to build dwellings and canoes. Rushes were used to make mats and bags. When the French first became acquainted with these tribes, the French noted that the Algonquin used almost 275 different species of plants for medicine, 130 for food, and

■ *A forest-dwelling Algonquin mixes a pot of medicine. Algonquin medicine men used a wide variety of plant species to create their remedies.*

25 for dyes. Each spring, they tapped maple trees to make syrup and sugar.

The northern woodland tribes were generally divided into groups, or bands. Each group controlled its own hunting territory and was independent of other groups. They were made up of a number of related families, and seldom exceeded four hundred people. In theory, every individual in the group was equal. Their leader, usually someone who had won that position through a display of courage, strength of character, or skill in hunting, enjoyed few, if any, special privileges.

It was these seminomadic tribes that first taught long-distance wilderness travel and woodland hunting to the whites. If it had not been for the durable but light canoes that woodland natives perfected, it is doubtful whether the French fur traders of the seventeenth and eighteenth centuries would have been able to roam so widely. Fur-trade routes eventually extended from Montreal all the way to the Pacific.

The Farming Tribes

In contrast to the woodland tribes, the Huron and Iroquoian people in central and eastern Canada mainly relied on agriculture for their survival, although they also did some hunting and fishing. Because of this, they were able to settle in areas for much longer periods of time and their social structure was considerably different.

Unlike other First Nations, where the burden of livelihood rested with the males, here it was the women who provided most of the food. As a result, society revolved around the women. The fields, produce, longhouses, and children therefore belonged to them. The efficiency of this social system allowed the men to organize democratic systems of government and to wage war.

The Iroquoian-speaking Huron tribe, which lived in what is now southwestern Ontario, obtained as much as 75 percent of their food by farming. They ate primarily corn, beans, squash, and sunflower seeds, and supplemented their

■ Native Longhouses

The Huron, like other Iroquoian tribes, lived in longhouses, wooden buildings about two hundred feet long and covered in rough bark. Longhouses had no windows, but they had holes in the top to let out smoke and allow some sunlight in. Inside, fires for cooking and warmth were kept burning day and night. Longhouses were home to a number of extended families and were built as part of stockaded villages where as many as fifteen hundred to twenty-five hundred people, or ten to thirty families, lived together. Villages were located close to the fields where the crops were tended. A new village site was sought roughly once every ten years, when all the easily accessible land had been used up.

At the Lawson Prehistoric Indian Village in London, Ontario, visitors can view Canada's only ongoing excavation and reconstruction of a prehistoric village. Elm longhouses are being reconstructed there according to historic descriptions and the floor plan recovered during excavation. The Lawson longhouses housed some fifteen hundred Neutral Indians five hundred years ago. Longhouse replicas can also be found among the re-created historic buildings at Sainte-Marie among the Huron, the site of a 1640s Jesuit mission village (Ontario's first European community) and Huron settlement on the Georgian Bay, near Midland.

■ *A replica of a traditional Iroquoian longhouse.*

diet with fish and with game such as venison (deer meat). The Iroquois had developed various means of food preparation and storage. The produce of the fields was dried and hung from the ceilings of their dwellings for storage. Fish were either sun-dried or smoked and then packed in bark containers.

The men cleared new farmland by chopping down trees and cutting the brush, then burning undergrowth and tree stumps that could not be removed easily. The planting, tending, and harvesting of crops was done by the women. They used hoes, made from moose antlers or deer shoulder blades, to pile the earth into mounds. They then used digging sticks to make a hole an inch or so deep in each mound to sow seeds.

Hunting Parties

Whereas farming was considered entirely the domain of women, fishing and hunting were largely male activities. Fishing was more important, because fish provided the major source of protein. The Huron organized a month-long fishing expedition to Georgian Bay each fall to obtain spawning white fish.

Although the hunt provided less food than farming and fishing, it was important because hides and pelts were needed for clothing. The Huron mounted autumn and late-winter deer hunting expeditions, usually consisting of several hundred men. Their search for game often took them on lengthy journeys south or east of their homes. During the late-winter hunt, a few women would accompany the men to assist with the butchering and preparation of hides. Because venison did not preserve well, some cuts were smoked, but most of the meat obtained on a deer hunt was eaten immediately. The fat and the hides, however, were always brought home to the villages.

Many of the Algonquin Nations integrated spiritual beliefs into their hunting practices. The bear, for example, was treated with particular respect. A hunter would talk or sing to the bear before killing it, assuring the animal that its death was required only because the hunter and his family needed food. As a mark of respect, the skulls of bears and beavers were carefully cleaned and then placed high on a pole or in a tree where dogs could not chew on them. Certain practices were believed to reinforce the relationship between hunters and animal spirits. Hunters might carry charms to help in hunting, such as beaks, claws, or a weasel's skull.

Trade Between First Nations

The Algonquin and Iroquois Nations interacted via networks of kinship, trade, and sometimes war. Northern Iroquois, such as the Huron, produced sizeable surpluses of corn and tobacco, but fur and game were in short supply. The Algonquin, on the other hand, prized corn. Thus, these peoples exchanged surplus corn for the products of the hunt. The amounts were small, but the routes and methods of trade were well established and goods and information were exchanged long before the Europeans entered the scene. Generally, the group whose members first developed a given trade route had the rights to it. But they could lease these rights, or even transfer them to other groups.

It is estimated that as many as a quarter of a million native people lived in present-day Canada when French explorers first arrived there in the early 1600s, and that approximately sixty thousand of these people lived in the area that we now know as Ontario. Some of these First Nations people had formed complex societies with permanent dwellings and democratic political customs. As accomplished and powerful as these nations were, however, they were to find themselves facing desperate challenges in the coming years, not only from the newly arrived French and later the British but also from deepening conflicts with each other.

The Europeans Arrive

When the earliest Europeans arrived, very few were interested in the land as a place to settle and farm. What they mainly came for was fur. By the 1600s, fur-bearing animals had become scarce in Europe, and finding a new and plentiful source was of vital importance. European explorers were quick to realize that the New World contained plenty of wild animals with useful fur, especially beavers. An adult beaver averages about fifty pounds, and an estimated 16 million of them lived in North America in the early 1600s. Although beavers were the cornerstone of the early Canadian fur trade, as trappers spread out from Quebec and present-day Ontario into western Canada, they also began to trade in fishers, wolverines (known as a tough animal to trap because it often stole bait or wrecked traps), kit fox, and snowshoe hares.

Because beavers were relatively easy to catch and kill, by the late 1600s nearly one hundred thousand beaver pelts were being traded out of the New World each year. Fur traders

■ *Native Canadians exchange furs for rifles with French traders.*

recruited the people of the First Nations to help find and collect furs for them. They were eager to use the hunting skills of tribes like the Ojibwa and Algonquin, which had been doing this for hundreds of years. Because the native people wanted the white man's iron pots and tools in exchange, the trade was mutually agreeable. Eventually, First Nations people collected furs not only for British traders of the Hudson's Bay Company, the powerful fur-trading monopoly chartered by King Charles II of England in 1670, but also for French traders. The latter were among the earliest explorers of what the French in Quebec called the Pays d'en Haut—the "upper country" that eventually became Ontario. Native peoples also served as auxiliary soldiers when the British and the French went to war. Over time, native traders became more and more dependent on metal tools, muskets, and other trade goods brought in by the Europeans.

Natives Become Astute Traders

The account books of the Hudson's Bay Company show that, contrary to popular belief, native people did not part with their furs frivolously for cheap trinkets. They spent most of their trading and trapping income on firearms, ammunition, metal goods, cloth, blankets, tobacco, and brandy. In addition to demanding quality merchandise, they had very specific design requirements. For example, they wanted lightweight and durable hunting and trapping equipment, a real challenge for European manufacturers.

The kettle had an immediate impact on the daily lives of native women. For the first time, they had a durable, transportable vessel that could be used over an open fire. As a result, they no longer had to boil water by placing heated

■ Europe's Deadly Imports

Unfortunately for Native North American societies, when the Europeans began to arrive in force in the mid-1600s they did not bring along merely iron pots and woolen blankets. They also brought with them the distilled alcohol and the germs that would prove to pose deadly long-term problems for native societies.

Alcohol was probably the single-most disruptive of all the new commodities introduced by whites. It ruined the lives of thousands who became addicted to it and continues to be a problem for the people of Ontario's First Nations today. Some researchers have suggested that Native North Americans have a genetic makeup that increases the risk of alcoholism. Another theory points to cultural factors, especially the lack of rituals and existing social controls when a society is suddenly exposed to a potent drug like alcohol. (Another example is how opium similarly devastated the Chinese when the British introduced it to them early in the nineteenth century.)

As destructive a disease as alcoholism is, it paled in its deadliness next to infectious diseases such as smallpox. Native North Americans had not been able to build up some resistance to these diseases, as had Europeans who had been exposed to them for centuries. Thus, smallpox was able to infect and wipe out virtually entire tribes in the New World. For example, a survey of thirty-two Huron villages in 1639 counted just twelve hundred inhabitants, whereas a decade or so before there had been about thirty thousand.

In most cases Europeans unintentionally infected Indians, though the disease was also used as a weapon of war and even a means of genocide. Lee Sultzman relates what happened to a tribe of Ottawa based in the area of present-day Ontario and Michigan in the 1760s after opposing the British. The Ottawa "remember a mysterious tin box given them by British traders shortly after the war, which they were told not to open until they got back to their villages. They did as instructed, but there was nothing inside other than a strange brown powder. Immediately afterwards, an especially deadly smallpox epidemic broke out which decimated their villages."

stones in it. European blankets were also popular, as were cotton and woolen goods. They may not have been as warm as fur, but these materials dried more quickly and wool provided warmth even when wet. The metal knives, needles, and scissors provided by the Europeans made it much easier to cut and sew hides and pelts into clothing.

Firearms were also in high demand, for several reasons. Traditionally, native hunters had stalked and killed game at close range with bows and arrows or lances. One shortcoming of these methods was that the animal sometimes did not die immediately and the hunter might have to chase it for quite a long way before the animal finally bled to death. Firearms increased the likelihood of killing the animal quickly. Firearms were also important for self-defense and war.

Dueling Religions

The devout among the Catholic French saw the discovery of the New World as an opportunity to convert the "heathen natives" to Christianity. Among the first devoutly religious people who traveled to Canada to bring the word of God to the native people were members of a French order called the Recollets. Between 1625 and 1629, Jesuit missionaries started working alongside the Recollets, living and traveling with the native people and learning their languages.

At first the missionaries believed that the native people's religions were evil and that their shamans were "agents of the devil." European missionaries felt that all the old beliefs had to be driven out to create room for the "true faith." But as the priests began to understand more of the language and culture, they realized that native beliefs reflected an all-powerful God and an afterlife. The priests then tried to build on whatever beliefs were not in conflict with Christianity and eliminate the rest. Still, they did not find it easy to make converts.

"Do they hunt in heaven, or make war, or go to feasts?" a Jesuit priest was asked by a Huron warrior. When the priest replied that there was nothing earthly in the Christian heaven, the Huron man replied, "Then I will not go. It is no good to be lazy."[5]

Mission Among the Huron

In 1634, a Jesuit priest named Jean de Brebeuf and two other missionaries took over the "Mission Among the Huron" from the Recollets. Brebeuf decided to establish a permanent settlement, and in 1639 helped build the Sainte-Marie among the Huron mission near the Huron village of Ossossane, located near the present-day town of Midland.

The outer palisade of the mission surrounded two enclosures, one for the French, the other for the Huron. On the French side were residences and stables, a granary and workshops, and a chapel for the Jesuits. On the Huron side were more residences, a hospital, a cemetery, and a church. Outside the palisade lay cultivated fields.

Some Jesuit priests lived at Sainte-Marie while others stayed there to rest after tours to outlying Huron missions. Soldiers and fur traders also found lodging at the mission. The farmers and artisans of Sainte-Marie were called *donnés* (from the French "to give"). They were devout laypeople who donated their skills and years of their lives to the service of God.

By 1648, the three Jesuit priests at Sainte-Marie had four assistants working for them, in addition to twenty-three *donnés*, seven domestics, four boys, and eight soldiers. An additional fifteen priests lived at outpost missions elsewhere in the Huron territory, which was called Huronia.

Fighting the Beaver War

While the Jesuits were busy expanding their mission among the Huron, the French in Quebec had made the mistake of siding with the Huron and Algonquin against the Iroquois. This had incurred the wrath of the Iroquois, who not only wanted revenge, but more specifically, they wanted control of the expanding fur trade. The Iroquois decided to go to war, and in July 1648 they began raiding the outlying missions in Huronia. The first mission to be targeted was St. Joseph. The Jesuit priest there had just finished reading mass when Iroquois raiders struck. In the subsequent attack, the mission was wiped out and the church burned to the ground.

On March 15, 1649, Iroquois warriors overran two more missions. Among the prisoners taken was Brebeuf, who was later tortured to death. The Iroquois next reconnoitered around Sainte-Marie itself, and went on to burn other Huron villages in the area. The many attacks and deaths in Huronia as a result of the war with the Iroquois, which is also referred to as the Beaver War (because it was all about control of the fur trade), caused the Jesuits to abandon the fortress they had set up at Sainte-Marie. Before leaving in late 1649, they

burned the compound down themselves so it would not fall into the hands of the Iroquois.

The Huron who were left behind fled to islands in Georgian Bay and Lake Huron, where they tried to regroup with their allies and survive the winter. They had few supplies and were also relentlessly pursued by the Iroquois. In the early summer of 1650, forty well-armed Frenchmen set out from Montreal hoping to save Huronia, only to be met on the way by the remnants of the Huron Nation. These survivors, about three hundred in total, were relocated at Lorette, near Quebec, where their descendants still live today. Another one thousand Huron who had fled even farther west, to present-day Michigan and Wisconsin, combined with their allies, the Tobacco, to create a new tribe called the Wyandot. "Not only the Hurons," notes Robert Bothwell, "but all the nations of the Great Lakes region were affected, depopulating what is now southern Ontario and Michigan."[6]

The Beaver War continued for many years and thousands of native people died as a result of the hostilities. As the conflict spread, it involved more and more tribes in the Great Lakes area and beyond. The greed for furs, sparked by the arrival of the Europeans and fueled by age-old conflicts between

First Nations tribes, not only upset the balance of power but also disrupted a way of life that served Canada's native people for thousands of years.

Trading Furs with the English

Initially, Canada was settled mostly by the French, who had established a colony in the modern-day area of Quebec. The king of France had laid claim to much of the land in present-day Quebec and beyond, and the French had developed close ties with the native people who lived in those areas.

The French were mainly interested in two things: the fur trade and missionary work among the native people. Of the two, the first was by far the more important. But because the fur trade was so lucrative, other countries were also interested in gaining control of it and challenged France's claims. War had already broken out among the First Nations for this very reason.

During the Beaver War, in an attempt to appease the Iroquois, the French forbade their citizens to travel and trade outside specific areas. But in 1659 two young French fur traders, Pierre-Esprit Radisson and Médard Chouart des Groseilliers, ignored this law and explored Ontario far inland toward James Bay, all the way up the Ottawa River. They observed the complex network of waterways and conceived the idea that practical water links must exist between the Great Lakes and Hudson Bay. When they returned to Montreal, they were thrown in jail and fined by the governor of New France for traveling without his permission in the Pays d'en Haut.

■ *A woodcut sketch depicts a busy scene at a Hudson's Bay Company fur-trading store.*

Radisson and Groseilliers left the French colony in anger and offered their services to the British. In 1668–1669 they led an exploratory, British-backed voyage into James Bay. It was the successful outcome of this journey that resulted in King Charles II of England providing a charter to the Hudson's Bay Company in 1670. The company's official purpose included exploration as well as trade. It quickly proceeded to establish forts and strongholds on the bay whose name it bears. Places such as Moose Factory (the oldest white settlement in the area, founded in 1673) and Fort Albany, Ontario, started out as Hudson's Bay Company trading posts.

Initially the Hudson's Bay Company was in strong competition with the French fur traders, who had established La Compagnie du Nord in 1682. France and England were at war in Europe, and the animosities spilled over to Canada and North America. Between 1674 and 1713, the French and the British fought hard over who would have control of Hudson Bay, its surrounding lands, and the fur trade. By the early 1700s, it looked like the French had regained control. But then in 1713, the Treaty of Utrecht ended the war between France and England in Europe as well as in North America. The treaty called for the French to return to the Hudson's Bay Company all the trading posts, forts, and lands the French had taken during the war. From that point on, the British consolidated control of the area and the Hudson's Bay Company would own much of the present-day Canadian north until well into the nineteenth century.

Rapid Changes on the Way

The First Nations had survived for thousands of years on their land, in the harshest of climates and circumstances. They had built largely democratic, well-organized societies. They had established religions and workable technologies for survival—technologies that the Europeans in some cases did, and in other cases, should have, learned from when they first stepped off their ships. The centuries that followed almost swallowed up the people and culture of the First Nations in Canada, as the French and English fought over the colonies. Eventually, their descendants joined forces to face the world as a new country and learn to coexist more peacefully.

A Loyalist Stronghold

A s the area of present-day Ontario began to be populated with people of English descent, its inhabitants vacillated between joining forces with the people in French-speaking Quebec and going their own way. In the end, nudged along by the possibility of being swallowed up by the newly formed United States to the south, the people of Ontario set aside their differences and decided to join forces with Quebec and the other provinces to become uniquely Canadian.

A Vast and Empty Land

With the exception of the Jesuit missions in the early half of the 1600s, the land immediately to the west of Quebec was not really settled by Europeans until the second half of the eighteenth century. By that time, the area's white population (fewer than 150,000) was mostly French and lived along the St. Lawrence River in Quebec. While the French traded and hunted in the Pays d'en Haut that lay to their west, it was the English-speaking races that eventually settled there.

The American War of Independence (1775–1781) provided further impulse for Ontario's settlement. During this struggle, American colonials who supported the British were called Loyalists. Mobs of American rebels were known to beat and even murder some Loyalists. Soon after "the shot heard round the world" in the battle at Lexington, Massachusetts, that started the war on April 19, 1775, thousands of Loyalists began to flee into Britain's Canadian colonies. This influx

continued even after the war had ended.

Initially, about seven thousand Loyalists moved to the banks of the St. Lawrence River and the shores of Lake Erie and Lake Ontario, all of which was Quebec at the time. After this wave came the so-called "late Loyalists," Americans who, in order to obtain free land, claimed they had been loyal to Britain. Behind them came thousands of ordinary American pioneers, who ignored political boundaries in the search for new land. It is estimated that more than fifty thousand people moved from colonial America into parts of present-day Canada as a result of the war and the subsequent shift in power. "Unknown to many today," note the authors of *Canada*, "not all were of British descent—they represented a mix of ethnic backgrounds. Regardless, their arrival strengthened Great Britain's hold on this part of its empire."[7]

■ *Bloody scenes such as this one from the Battle of Bunker Hill compelled many Loyalists to flee into neighboring Ontario during the American War of Independence.*

Early European Immigrants

Because most of the best St. Lawrence River valley land was already in the hands of French Canadians, the new arrivals had to look elsewhere. Thousands ended up settling in Nova Scotia, the British colony north of colonial New Hampshire (present-day Maine). In response to this immigration, in 1784 the British split Nova Scotia in half to create the new colony of New Brunswick. Many other Loyalists began to congregate in the Great Lakes–St. Lawrence lowlands of Quebec. To stimulate settlement, the British government offered "Crown Land," which was available for sixpence per acre plus survey costs and an oath of allegiance. As a result, other European settlers began arriving, too. German settlers, for example, were being actively recruited as early as 1750. They settled largely in the fertile agricultural region surrounding Canada's

"German capital," the town of Berlin (present-day Kitchener). In this area the German and the British flags flew side by side, and in the mid–nineteenth century Queen Victoria's and the kaiser's birthdays were celebrated as civic holidays.

In time, more and more settlers arrived in the Great Lakes–St. Lawrence lowlands, some in organized groups. Others were brought in by land-development firms such as the Canada Company. These settlers were assigned farms owned by the company. Sometimes, whole communities moved north to Quebec. A group of Dutch Pennsylvanians, for example, settled in present-day Kitchener. It was also common for men who worked for the Hudson's Bay Company's outposts far north to settle their families in southern towns. The men, most of them English or Scottish, would then "commute" back and forth.

Settling Upper Canada

In 1784, a group of about five thousand English Loyalists began to clear the forests in the "upper Canada" region west of the Ottawa River to establish farms. The land had not yet been surveyed, and the Loyalists had to live in tents until it was. They had few supplies, seeds, or tools, and the first winter especially was challenging:

> The first task was to build a log shanty to provide shelter for the first winter. These huts were small, only 10 or 12 feet long, built of round logs, and frequently with only a hole in the roof to serve as a chimney. This crude beginning was followed by labourious clearing of the land, building of a log house, and cultivation of the virgin soil. All of these advances were accomplished with extreme hardship, primitive tools, great determination, and faith in British institutions.[8]

Fortunately, many of the Loyalist settlers were frontier farmers, tough and skilled in the subsistence life that confronted them. The British government supplied each family with small rations of flour, pork, beef, salt, and butter. Eventually they also all received an ax, a spade, and a hoe. Other tools, such as scythes and plows, were shared between families.

The First Nations people who lived in the area taught the new arrivals how to convert deerskin into boots and jackets. The settlers grew flax to be turned into rough linen for clothes. They planted apple orchards and raised sheep. A gristmill had been built in Niagara and another was soon added at present-day Napanee, farther north on the shores of Lake Ontario. Settlers unable to reach such mills used portable, hand-operated units or ground their grain with wooden pestles.

Building a New Province

With Loyalist settlers becoming established, the culture clash between French and British settlers increased. In 1791, the British Parliament passed the Constitutional Act to help address this conflict. The act divided the colony of Quebec into two parts, Upper and Lower Canada, corresponding to today's provinces of Ontario and Quebec. (The immense area in the vicinity of Hudson Bay, so-called Rupert's Land, was owned by the Hudson's Bay Company and did not become part of Ontario and Quebec until the company sold the land to the new nation of Canada in 1870.) Lower Canada remained overwhelmingly French, but Upper Canada had an English-speaking majority. It was to have its own legislature and the language, law, and religion desired by the newly enlarged English-speaking community.

John Graves Simcoe, a dynamic Englishman who had led a Loyalist regiment in the war against America, was appointed as Upper Canada's governor. His plan was to establish a system of government that was modeled on Britain's. Simcoe's cabinet consisted of an Executive Council made up of leading citizens. There was also a Legislative Council modeled on the British House of Lords, though the council's members were appointed, not hereditary. The only elected body was the Legislative Assembly. The governor was responsible to the British government back in London, but not to the Legislative Assembly or the people he ruled. Settling land was the major government business.

Only a handful of the pioneer settlers of Upper Canada were qualified to hold government positions. These few founded the dynasties that came to be known collectively as "the Family Compact." Land was the main source of wealth and power at the time. Because members also held government positions, these few could make large land grants to themselves, thus securing not only their own position, but also that of their descendants. The Family Compact, though a private group, controlled Ontario well into the twentieth century.

Simcoe traveled across his vast domain by canoe and snowshoe, setting former British soldiers to work. They built roads that still exist today, such as Yonge Street, which ran

from Lake Ontario to Lake Simcoe, and Dundas, which ran from Dundas to London, and later to York. Simcoe also had defenses fortified against a possible American attack. He planned new towns in his territory, and renamed existing ones with English names (Newark for Niagara, York for Toronto). He picked a wilderness site to be the capital for the new province; he called it London and its river the Thames. But he was overruled and ordered to make York the capital instead. (York would revert to its original name of Toronto in 1834.)

Simcoe knew that he needed to develop more land, but to do that he needed more people. New immigrants were arriving all the time, including many from America. Some Americans came solely to speculate in land; they would obtain it for free, then sell it and head home. Others stayed, but were doubted by the old timers for years. Soon the new American, English, Irish, Scottish, and German immigrants outnumbered the early Loyalists. Within three generations, the new province had half the number of inhabitants that the thirteen American colonies had on the eve of the American Revolution.

■ A contemporary engraving portrays fishermen and stevedores at work on a Toronto quay. John Graves Simcoe chose Toronto, then called York, as the capital of Upper Canada.

Wars Shape Upper Canada

The threat of military invasion posed by its unpredictable neighbor to the south helped to unite the people of Upper Canada. Military invasion, however, was not the only threat.

■ The Lumber Industry

Forestry was Canada's biggest industry during most of the nineteenth century, mainly driven by the Royal Navy and British shipbuilding boom. In the Ottawa River valley, and in other valleys in Canada East and West, as many as twenty-five thousand lumbermen were employed by 1864 in various jobs. Cruisers picked the best timber stands and swampers broke trail and cleared the camp area while others built a caboose, a log cabin in which up to fifty men would live. The log cabin had no windows and a fire was kept going night and day. Smoke escaped through an opening in the roof. Lumbermen ate three meals a day, typically consisting of pork, beans, tea, and a cup of melted pork fat to counter the winter cold. Whiskey was forbidden in the camps.

Skillful axmen worked in pairs, using razor-sharp twelve-pound axes, taking alternate swings at a tree. Once felled, the tree was cut into forty-foot lengths and the logs were then squared into so-called "Ottawa sticks." As soon as the spring breakup of river ice occurred, logs were floated down the rivers and lakes into the St. Lawrence in three-hundred-by-sixty-foot rafts, which were held together with birch saplings.

As many as eight smaller rafts were chained into one huge raft of up to one hundred thousand cubic feet. The men guiding these rafts lived on board. It was risky work. These "white watermen," using long handspikes as tools, routinely risked their lives as jam breakers, chopping or rolling key logs free and often having to scramble to safety across the seething jumble of wood with just seconds to spare.

The United States was also the source of an almost constant civilian invasion. Emigration from New York and other states created a steady influx of Americans into southern Canada, raising the possibility that part of Canada could start to identify with the United States and clamor for statehood. This is, after all, more or less how Mexico lost Texas to the United States in the 1830s.

Britain's Canadian colonies faced a crisis when America again declared war on Britain on June 18, 1812, after a long-simmering dispute over trade and other issues. In addition to fighting the British, Americans set their sights on conquering Canada. To the Americans, this seemed a logical and easy conquest and many believed that Canadians would adjust and learn to live under the Stars and Stripes. The half a million people living in Canada at this time were thinly spread out in the maritime colonies and Lower and Upper Canada.

They were not sure what they wanted. Some were Loyalists, staunchly true to the English king; many were recent immigrants, their homes in Canada but their hearts still in America. Nearly two-thirds of Canada's population was French and they had no love for England at all, the eldest still able to remember the painful days of 1763 when France had been forced to cede most of its North American possessions to the British.

The Americans' most immediate objective was Montreal, from which they could control the St. Lawrence River, Upper and Lower Canada's vital supply route. But America's aggressiveness ultimately drove French and English Canadians to work together to defend their homeland. Militarily, the British and Canadians were outnumbered. At the start of the war, some eight thousand British and Canadian regulars and less than twenty thousand militia faced thirty-five thousand American regulars and a militia of hundreds of thousands.

Isaac Brock to the Rescue

In the face of this opposition, Canadians needed a good leader and they found him in Major General Isaac Brock. He was the administrator for the government of Upper Canada, but also spoke fluent French and mingled easily in Lower Canada. A tall, broad-shouldered, and muscular man, Brock had been a soldier for twenty-six years and commander in Canada since 1802. He was utterly fearless and yet uncommonly kind. For example, he insisted that his men have warm greatcoats and cancelled parades on frigid days.

General Brock gained immediate glory in August 1812 by defeating a larger American force under General William Hull at Detroit. In October of the same year Canadian forces also beat back an American attack at Queenston Heights on the Niagara River. This victory proved costly for the British, however, as an American sharpshooter killed Brock. Brock's tomb in Queenston today commemorates his heroism. Nearby is another site of national pride: the restored house, now a museum, in which Laura Secord overheard American plans for the attack. She walked nineteen miles (thirty kilometers) to warn the British of the impending attack, allowing them to organize a victorious ambush.

The Americans were more successful in 1813. In April, they attacked and captured York, Upper Canada's capital. Just three hundred British regulars, three hundred militiamen,

and one hundred natives were defending York. When the Canadians realized they were completely outnumbered and unable to defend the town, they decided to blow up their ammunition dump, which contained four hundred barrels of gunpowder. The resulting explosion killed three hundred American invaders, who burned down York's legislative building and looted the town in retaliation. Although the Americans retreated eleven days later, York was left in ruins. At the Battle of the Thames River in October 1813, American forces won a victory in which the famous native Shawnee leader Tecumseh, allied with the British and Canadians, was killed. Ultimately, however, French and English Canadians, joined by native people, successfully fought side by side to thwart the American invasion.

■ *A portrait of Major General Isaac Brock, the commander of British forces in Canada during the War of 1812.*

Losing the Peace?

The War of 1812 was ended on December 24, 1814, when the Treaty of Ghent was signed in Belgium. Although both sides claimed to have won the war, Canadian/British forces had managed to capture some American territory. The treaty, however, determined that all captured land had to be returned to the Americans. The treaty restored the previous status quo, but key decisions on fishing rights, naval forces in the Great Lakes, and national borders were postponed. The old boundary, the 49th parallel, prevailed. In the end, this was a victory for the Americans.

In a sense, although Canada had won the war, it lost the peace. Some eighty-six hundred Canadians and Britons had died for no apparent gain and parts of Upper Canada had been left in ruins. But the Canadian spirit was tangible and strong for the first time. Upper Canadians, Lower Canadians, and Maritimers; Britons, French, and natives: They had all stood united. Having discovered common causes, people in Canada were more agreeable than ever to finding a workable way to unite without sacrificing their identities or ways of life. It was really the beginning of the Canadian nation.

■ *The American frigate* Constitution *sinks the British warship* HMS Guerriere *off the coast of Newfoundland during the War of 1812.*

The Two Sides of British Rule

After the War of 1812 ended, the population of Upper Canada began to grow rapidly. During the 1820s, towns including Bytown (present-day Ottawa) became prosperous centers of trade. Cities were taking root along the shores of Lake Ontario and Lake Erie. Mills, canals, small factories, and roads were built. The Trent, Rideau, and the first Welland Canals date from this time. Large groups of immigrants, mostly from England, Scotland, and Ireland, came to Ontario after these improvements had been made.

But even though Canada was growing and becoming more united, it was not at all independent—the British government still ruled it as a colony. In Upper Canada, the governmental system first established by Simcoe remained in effect throughout the first half of the nineteenth century. The Family Compact continued to wield much power and engaged in patronage and favoritism. These privileged individuals owned much of the best uncultivated land and prevented settlements there, disrupting the natural development of roads and other services. During the 1820s, Upper Canadians became increasingly upset with the state of affairs.

The Government Reforms

As the demand for government reform grew, leaders emerged. Robert Baldwin, a lawyer, led the reformers in Upper Canada.

In Lower Canada, the movement was led by Louis-Hippolyte La Fontaine. Baldwin and La Fontaine formed an important English-French alliance on the basis that, by working together as Canadians, they could change things for the better.

Both the British and colonial governments ignored these demands for political reform at first, with political scandals and corruption continuing. In an attempt to win over the reformers, the British appointed a new governor of Upper Canada, Sir Francis Bond Head, in 1835. But Head adopted a confrontational attitude with the reformers and even dissolved the reform-dominated Legislative Assembly.

Head's vendetta against the reformers alienated moderates and fanned the flames of revolt. The growing dissent erupted into rebellion in Upper Canada in late 1837, led by William Mackenzie, a newspaperman and member of the assembly. He organized a group of about one thousand armed farmers and workers, but government soldiers quickly dispersed them. Several rebels were killed, some imprisoned, and others, including Mackenzie, fled to the United States.

Uprisings continued into 1838, both in Upper and Lower Canada. Concerned about all the commotion, the British authorities sent Lord Durham to Canada to look into the fundamental cause of the discontent. Durham presented his report in 1839, claiming the main problem could be traced to fundamental differences between the British and French societies. Durham's solution was to anglicize the French Canadians. To accomplish this, he proposed the political union of Upper and Lower Canada. He did also report on government mismanagement (power was concentrated, he said, in the hands of "a petty, corrupt, insolent Tory clique"[9]) and recommended that Canada be given an administration consisting of elected representatives who were responsible to the people.

Unity with Lower Canada

The British Parliament believed that responsible government was equivalent to independence, which they would not approve. The British did agree, on the other hand, to unite the two colonies. The Act of Union was ratified in 1840, and activated in 1841, uniting Upper and Lower Canada into a single colony called the Province of Canada. Even so, a distinction was retained: Upper Canada was renamed Canada West, and Lower Canada became Canada East.

And so it was that the first joint Canadian Assembly met in June 1841, with La Fontaine and Baldwin acting as co-premiers. The new province's capital was initially in Kingston, but was moved to Montreal in 1843. The new assembly had a difficult time resolving issues, however, and in practice its members usually voted along party lines. This resulted in bitter conflicts between the English and the French, and made it hard for the new government to be effective.

The British government continued to control the country. But in 1847, the British colonial office finally conceded that it was neither possible nor desirable to carry on the government of any of the British provinces in North America in opposition to the opinion of the inhabitants. In 1848, the joint colony was made self-governing in all matters except foreign affairs.

Concurrent with these political changes, Britain had decided to adopt a policy of free trade, spelling trouble for Canada. Britain had always controlled its colonial business through the use of tariffs (taxes on imported or exported goods). Tariffs had protected Canadian products from competitors in the British market. As part of the shift to free trade, Britain began progressively wiping out these tariffs between 1846 and 1849. No longer would the colonies enjoy special treatment in Britain. From then on, their goods would have to compete on equal terms with those from Europe and the United States. The removal of the protective walls behind which Canadian businesses had developed was a serious blow for the Canadian economy and led to immediate financial hardship for many.

Civil Unrest Shakes Canada West

During the 1848 election, the Reform Party swept into power with decisive majorities in both Canada East and West. The great Reform Ministry, the first true one-party cabinet, took office in March 1848. Once again, La Fontaine and Baldwin led the government as a team. Responsible government by party had arrived at last.

The Reform Ministry tried to compensate the victims of the 1837–1838 rebellions when it passed the Rebellion Losses Bill. It proposed to award tens of thousands of dollars in damages to victims in Canada West, and recommended that Canada East victims be similarly reimbursed. La Fontaine's proposal staggered the conservative Tories—the old English ruling class, who were still firmly entrenched. Although

■ *A drawing depicts nineteenth-century Montreal. The city was chosen as the capital of the Province of Canada in 1843, but lost the distinction to Ottawa in 1867.*

La Fontaine agreed that anyone exiled or convicted of participation in rebellion would not be compensated, it was common knowledge that many rebels had never been brought to trial.

The Tories felt betrayed and predicted civil war. In 1849, riots and civil unrest erupted across Canada. Groups of English Canadians in Montreal, where more than half of the fifty-five thousand residents were English-speaking, rioted for four months. Mobs burned down the Parliament House in Montreal. In one incident, La Fontaine had to be rescued by soldiers when he was attacked. Violence and demonstrations spread to Toronto, Bytown, and Hamilton.

The Tories, who in 1837 had accused the rebels of treason for trying to introduce an American system of government into Canada, now proposed to join the United States. They published their Annexation Manifesto in Montreal in October 1849. It was signed by 325 of the leading figures in Montreal society, many of whom were dismayed by the collapse of Canadian business following Britain's shift to free trade. Even though lucrative new markets would open up to Canadian producers by joining the United States, other considerations swayed public opinion. Many French Canadians feared that

■ How Ottawa Came to Be the Capital

It would have been easy for Britain's Queen Victoria to overlook Ottawa when she decided in 1857 to pick the capital of the colony of Canada. After all, Ottawa as such was only two years old at the time, having been renamed in 1855 from its original Bytown. The name Ottawa was appropriate because it is the name of a local Indian tribe and means "to trade." Bytown had been named after John By, who directed the construction of the Rideau Canal from 1826 to 1832. Linked by the Rideau to Lake Ontario, Bytown began to flourish. It slowly developed into an important stop on the popular fur-trade route from the interior to Montreal, some 100 miles (160 kilometers) west of Bytown and not far from where the Ottawa River flows into the St. Lawrence.

Although Bytown kept growing into the 1850s as a center for the lumber trade to England and the United States, by the time of its rechristening as Ottawa the city was still a relatively minor one compared to Montreal and Toronto. But this minor status was exactly what made the politically astute Victoria name it as capital. She needed to make a choice because between 1840, when the British had reunited Upper and Lower Canada into the Province of Canada, and 1857, the capital had shifted among Kingston, Toronto, Montreal, and Quebec City. The people of Canada East wanted the capital to be Montreal or Quebec. The people of Canada West wanted it to be Kingston or Toronto. Faced with the constant bickering, Victoria chose sleepy Ottawa, right on the border of the two.

Many people received the news of the choice with incredulity. One wag joked that it was a good choice because the capital would never be invaded, since any invaders would get hopelessly lost in the woods before ever finding the city. But Ottawa was accepted and in 1867, when the Canadian colonies united to form the Dominion of Canada, Ottawa was the logical choice to become national capital.

their culture would be swallowed up as a part of the United States. In the end, the vast majority of French Canadians decided against this plan. The idea of Canada as a separate nation had survived once again.

The Final Steps to Confederation

Over the next fifteen years or so, the rebellions died down and Canada continued to expand. People in the United Provinces began to look more seriously at the idea that they should unite with the Maritime Provinces to establish their own independent country, separate from Britain. Beginning in September of

1864, they organized several conferences to discuss this idea, which eventually led to the creation of the Dominion of Canada. On July 1, 1867, guns saluted, soldiers marched, and the colonies of Ontario, Quebec, New Brunswick, and Nova Scotia officially became the first four provinces of Canada. (Newfoundland and Prince Edward Island voted against joining at the time.) Sir John A. Macdonald was sworn in as Canada's first prime minister and Ottawa remained the new nation's capital.

Expansion and Prosperity

Following the formation of the confederation, Canada's economy grew rapidly. Farming and industry expanded and Canadian scientists and inventors made advancements in many different fields. The government encouraged the exploration of the country's abundant natural resources, such as coal, iron, copper, and nickel. Other industries, such as shipping and forestry, also prospered. In Ontario, lumbering remained a major source of income and employment and was extended farther north.

Macdonald's government focused on building infrastructure, such as roads, canals, and railroads. During the 1880s, the Canadian government financed the building of the Canadian Pacific Railway, which by the end of the decade linked Vancouver on the west coast with Saint John on the east. In Ontario the Canadian Pacific ran west from Ottawa through Sudbury and then across the mostly uninhabited forests skirting Lake Superior to Thunder Bay. From there a 375-mile (600-kilometer) leg connected it to Winnipeg, Manitoba. At the same time many canals were added to Ontario's network of waterways.

Within larger cities, electrically powered streetcars were replacing horse-drawn ones. Initially, power lines were buried under the roads, but whenever it rained, the whole system would short-circuit. John Wright of Toronto solved this problem by inventing overhead cable, thereby changing the shape of the world's major cities. With fast public transport now easily available, people no longer had to live within walking distance of their jobs. Residential districts developed away from the noisy city factories.

Mineral Wealth

The true wealth of the Canadian Shield, the richest treasure of minerals in Canada, was first revealed when nickel and copper deposits were discovered while the Canadian Pacific Railway was being built north of Lake Superior. In 1883, railway workers discovered rich nickel-copper deposits near Sudbury. Significant mining did not begin until after 1892, when a viable process for separating copper was developed. By the early twentieth century, Sudbury was the world's largest producer of nickel. In 1894, iron ore deposits were discovered along the Ontario shore of Lake Superior. But this was only the beginning. In Ontario, the silver mines of Cobalt were opened in 1903, and the gold mines of Porcupine Lake and Kirkland Lake in 1908 and 1911, respectively.

North America's first commercially drilled oil well was sunk in Canada West, on the Ontario Peninsula between Lake Erie and Lake Huron, in 1857—one year before the more famous oil strike in Drake, Pennsylvania. The Canadian developer, James Williams, next built North America's first refinery to process the crude petroleum. A boomtown, appropriately named Oil Springs, quickly sprang up. For a short time in the 1860s and 1870s, Oil Springs's oil fields were among the most important in North America.

■ Alexander Graham Bell's First Phone

Scottish-born Alexander Graham Bell grew up near Brantford, Ontario. In the summer of 1874, home on a visit from Boston where he worked as a speech therapist, the twenty-seven-year-old Bell had the idea that became the basis of the telephone. It took him two years to build his first telephone. On August 3, 1876, in a Dominion Telegraph office at Mount Pleasant, Ontario, he heard his uncle David, two miles away in the telegraph office in Brantford, recite Shakespeare's famous lines from *Hamlet* beginning with "To be or not to be." This was the first intelligible telephone transmission from one building to another. One week later the first "long distance" call was made from Brantford to Paris, Ontario, eight miles to the northwest.

By November 1877 the newly established Bell Telephone Company of Canada had four subscribers. The fifth was Macdonald's successor as prime minister, Alexander Mackenzie, who wanted a telephone link between his office and the governor's general residence. This was installed and the company obligingly predated the prime minister's application to make him officially the first subscriber. Perhaps it was not such a good idea, however: The governor's wife, Lady Dufferin, was in the habit of sending her friend over to Mackenzie's office so she could sing to her over the phone!

Postwar Recovery

The start of World War II in 1939 helped Canada climb out of the economic depression it had slid into during the 1930s. In the process, Canada became one of the world's industrial giants. Canadian farms fed Allied forces overseas; manufacturing almost doubled as Canadian factories, many of them located in Ontario, expanded to produce goods previously imported from Britain. Many factories were retooled to produce the instruments of war: four hundred ships, sixty-five hundred tanks, and sixteen thousand aircraft.

After WWII, the young nation increasingly turned to its southern neighbor, especially following major investments made by American individuals and companies in Canada that totaled $10 billion by 1954. U.S. companies by then owned or controlled most of Canada's oil, gas, rubber, and automobile production; the majority of its nickel, iron, asbestos, and aluminum production; and over half of its pulp paper industry. The benefits to Ontario of short-range profits were obvious, but the long-term future for Ontario and the other provinces was not so good, as the country was becoming more and more dependent upon the United States so shortly after freeing itself from British control.

A High Standard of Living

The people of Ontario have come a long way in the last three centuries. From the people of the First Nations and the Loyalists to the immigrants that make up its diverse population today, Ontarians have always used the land's abundant natural resources to improve their lot. In time, they went from battling each other to restoring calm around the world as part of UN peace forces. In the process, the people of Ontario worked hard to build their society and today they enjoy among the highest standards of living in the world.

Life in Ontario Today

Life in Ontario is to a large extent determined by the environment, including the weather. The province boasts Canada's largest metropolitan area but also a seemingly limitless expanse of open countryside with many different types of landscape, from vineyards in the south to untamed wilderness in the north. The northwestern region has thousands of unspoiled lakes and rich, lush forests. Because four out of the five Great Lakes have part of their shores in Ontario, much of the province has scenic lakeside views and hundreds of miles of beautiful beaches. The Great Lakes also help keep the southern, populated section of the province somewhat warmer than the rest of Canada during the winter. During the summer months, it is sunny and warm enough to grow peach trees in the Niagara fruit belt.

This narrow, temperate zone in the vicinity of the Great Lakes and the St. Lawrence River is where some 90 percent of the inhabitants of Ontario live. This is also where most industry and commerce is located, much of it centered on the metropolis of Toronto, Ontario's thriving capital. The combination of a beautiful land, a diverse, hard-working population, and a varied economy has allowed the people of Ontario to establish an enviable lifestyle, by the standards of both Canada and the world.

A Province of Immigrants

Many of Ontario's more than 11 million inhabitants have immigrated to Canada from all over the world, beginning with the waves of British Loyalists that swept into southern

Canada during the American Revolution. Immigrants from France and Quebec helped create a French-speaking community along the eastern part of the present-day province. In the nineteenth and early twentieth centuries, workers from Scotland and Ireland were among the most common immigrants. After World War II, other European countries contributed more heavily to Ontario's immigration, especially Italy, Germany, Portugal, Greece, and Poland. Ontario also has significant concentrations of Chinese, Indians, West Indians, and East Asians.

Almost 60 percent of Canada's new immigrants settle in Ontario, where over one hundred languages and dialects are spoken today. Ontario also counts more than one hundred thousand people of aboriginal, métis (a person of mixed white—especially French—and Native North American descent), or Inuit origin. While English is the province's official language, the provincial government provides services in French to those regions where the Francophone (French-speaking) population is sufficiently high.

In Toronto, where the greatest ethnic diversity exists, the municipal government even prepares its annual property tax notices in six languages: English, French, Chinese, Italian, Greek, and Portuguese. The city boasts half-a-dozen Chinese newspapers. One Toronto radio station broadcasts in thirty different languages, and a television station broadcasts programs in a multiplicity of languages aimed at the city's specific ethnic communities, including movies in Urdu, an official language of Pakistan.

A Multifaceted Population

Although Ontario was established by people who tamed and farmed the land, today its inhabitants are no longer rural dwellers. Instead, almost 90 percent of them live in urban centers around the Great Lakes. Farming, of course, still plays an important role in the province. In the Ontario Peninsula, dairy producers, fruit growers, and other farmers produce as much as one-third of Canada's total agricultural output. Farther north, in the wilderness of the Canadian Shield, people live in small towns and cities and make a living harvesting the wealth of the forests and the mines.

But Ontario's heartbeat is strongest in its many metropolitan areas. The biggest cluster of these is located around Lake Ontario, from Saint Catharines, not far from Niagara Falls,

through Hamilton and Toronto and on to Oshawa. Often referred to as the "Golden Horseshoe," this is Canada's busiest manufacturing region and densest metropolitan area. The more than 6 million people who live in this region make it the most densely populated area in Canada, with nearly 250 people per square mile compared to the nationwide average of 7.8 (647 and 3.0 people per square kilometer). The second-largest metropolitan area in Ontario is Ottawa-Hull, where over a million people reside. For the most part, life in this part of Ontario is strongly influenced by America, and many of the residents work for companies at least partly owned by Americans. On the other hand, some towns, especially near the border with Quebec, still savor their French heritage.

The influence of dozens of cultures has shaped Ontario and made the province one of the most ethnically diverse areas in the world. Toronto is especially diverse, being home to almost one hundred different ethnic groups. It truly lives up to its suggested origin from a Huron word for "meeting place." One-third of Toronto's residents speak a language other than English at home. In 1997 alone, Toronto added eighty thousand immigrants from 169 countries to its population. They

■ *A nurse inspects a group of Scottish children onboard a ship bound for Canada. Ontario absorbed many such immigrants in search of opportunity and freedom.*

■ The Golden Horseshoe

The fifteen-city Golden Horseshoe is the fourth-largest metropolitan area in North America, having fewer residents than only New York City, Los Angeles, and Chicago. It is also one of the fastest-growing regions not only in Canada but in all of North America, adding residents at a faster rate than Los Angeles or Dallas.

The "golden" part of the name is due to both the area's farming and manufacturing. The fertile, brown, glacially deposited soil around Lake Ontario sustains a thriving agricultural industry including farms growing fruits, vegetables, and grains. The area is a center for dairy and beef cattle and also offers one of Canada's few opportunities for growing wine grapes. Manufacturing varies from the steel industry that dominates Hamilton to the auto plants of Oshawa and St. Catharines.

The Golden Horseshoe also owes its popularity to its proximity to the Welland Canal, a key link in the St. Lawrence Seaway trade route that was officially opened in 1959. The first Welland Canal was built in 1829 to bypass the Niagara River (and the Falls) and connect Lake Ontario to Lake Erie. Various route improvements and new locks have been built almost continuously over the last 175 years. The current Welland Canal is 27 miles (44 kilometers) long and drops or raises ships 330 feet (100 meters) between the shores of the two Great Lakes. Huge lake- and seagoing ships carry grain, iron ore, coal, and other cargoes from the Canadian heartland through the canal on their way to Atlantic ports. Manufactured items, steel, and produce from the Golden Horseshoe are also shipped west through the Welland on their way to Buffalo, Cleveland, Detroit, Chicago, and other Great Lakes port cities.

have helped to turn a city that was once somewhat dull into a lively and cosmopolitan place. Today, Toronto boasts one of the best multicultural festivals in the world. Considered the city's signature event, the Metro International Festival Caravan is held annually for nine days in mid-June. Events honor the city's diversity as dozens of ethnic communities are represented in international pavilions set up across Greater Toronto. The festival offers a multicultural display of art, music, dance, drama, food, and costumes.

Birth of a Multicultural Capital

Until the late eighteenth century, the site of present-day Toronto was a sparsely populated area on the north shore of

Lake Ontario. The lake was visited in 1615 by French explorer Etienne Brule, and by 1720 a trading post had been established called Fort Rouillé, later becoming known as Fort Toronto. But the French destroyed their own fort in 1759 so it would not fall into the hands of the British. Beginning in 1793, Lieutenant Governor John Simcoe reestablished Toronto in the new province of Upper Canada, renaming it York. Originally he intended it as a defense post against American attacks, but later the British colonial government ordered him to make it the provincial capital, which it has been ever since.

Today, Toronto is not only Ontario's capital, but also Canada's financial and administrative capital. More than 125,000 people are employed in its financial sector, which includes a stock exchange as well as headquarters for major banking and financial companies. Toronto is also Canada's gateway to the international marketplace. With the implementation of the North American Free Trade Agreement and increased reliance on trade in the last decade of the twentieth century, Toronto has become a hub for the distribution of goods, services, and people throughout the Western Hemisphere.

Toronto is sometimes referred to as the "Silicon Valley of the North" because seven of the top ten information technology companies are located there, including the Canadian

■ *A view of the twilight skyline of Toronto, Ontario's capital and the financial center of Canada.*

headquarters and research centers of Apple, Hewlett-Packard, and Sun Microsystems. Toronto has the fourth-highest concentration of commercial software companies in the world. The Toronto area also boasts one of the best telecommunications networks in the world, including one of the highest percentages of fiber optic cable installed, and more wireless phones per capita than anywhere in North America.

■ The Tower That Touches the Sky

Toronto's single most recognizable icon is the graceful CN Tower, which at 1,815 feet (553 meters) is more than a football-field taller than the world's tallest building (that is, a structure with floors all the way up) and almost twice the height of the Eiffel Tower. Although the CN Tower attracts more than 2 million visitors per year, it was not built solely for tourists. Rather, city officials in the early 1970s sought a solution to the communications problems the city was experiencing—the many new skyscrapers in Toronto were interfering with radio and television signals. The Canadian National Railway, long since branched out from building railroads to telecommunications and other businesses, decided to build a structure so tall that Toronto's communications problems would be solved for decades into the future.

The resulting CN Tower is a slender, needlelike tower made with three concrete legs that taper as they rise into the clouds. The doughnutlike SkyPod, a seven-story ring of observation decks, offices, restaurants, and stores, emerges at about eleven hundred feet. Above the SkyPod are more tower, a final observation deck, and the antennae and other high-tech communications equipment that have indeed provided city residents with exceptional radio and television reception. The tower is served by high-speed elevators and, for the superfit, a 2,579-step metal staircase. Engineers designed the structure to withstand 260-mile-per-hour winds and the average seventy-five lightning strikes it receives every year.

Opened in 1976, the CN Tower was an immediate hit with visitors and locals, who flocked to its observation decks (three indoor and one outdoor) and restaurants. A fine SkyPod restaurant rotates completely once every seventy-two minutes, providing diners with a stunning view that can reach seventy-five miles on a clear day. A recent addition to one SkyPod observation deck is a glass floor. Gazing straight down at city streets and SkyDome turf more than 1,000 feet below is an unsettling experience for many a visitor. More than 300 feet higher, at 1,465 feet, sits the world's highest public observation deck.

"New York Run by the Swiss"

The 4.5 million people who live in Greater Toronto have plenty of entertainment choices. Major League Baseball's Toronto Blue Jays and the Canadian Football League's Argonauts play in the spectacular SkyDome stadium, with its retractable roof. The city also boasts the Hockey Hall of Fame and the world famous Canadian National (CN) Tower, the tallest freestanding structure in the world and the center of telecommunications for Toronto.

For dedicated shoppers, the Toronto Underground features almost seven miles of continuous underground walkways that connect major office towers and hotels. This underground shopping center offers more than twelve hundred stores, restaurants, and entertainment centers. The walkways also connect the parliamentary buildings, the University of Toronto, and the Royal Ontario Museum. This underground system separates people from traffic and the weather and provides a very pleasant environment in which to shop, eat, work, and play.

Visitors are often surprised at how safe, clean, and orderly the city is, considering that so many cities in North America are quite the opposite. In 2000, Toronto's homicide rate per 100,000 residents was 2 and its robbery rate was 219. Compare that to such corresponding figures as 42 homicides and 585 robberies in Washington, D.C., or 34 and 978 in Atlanta. To find a safer city you have to go to one of Ontario's own small cities, like Sudbury (2 homicides and 74 robberies) and Windsor (4 and 72). The actor Peter Ustinov once memorably dubbed Toronto "New York run by the Swiss."[10] In a profile of Toronto, writer Richard Conniff noted, "Different ethnic groups and races mix congenially in a society structured on an old Anglo-Scottish ethos of order and propriety. The panhandlers, the strippers—and even the pale girl selling roses dipped in tar at a hip nightspot—are polite."[11]

A Diverse Economy and Job Market

Ontario generates some 40 percent of Canada's gross domestic product. Not surprisingly, it is the country's most productive province. Its manufacturing and service industries lead the way. Competitive advantages include Ontario's natural resources, the modern transportation system (including North America's largest public transit system after New York), a

■ A train speeds out of the Toronto train station. Ontario boasts the second largest public transit system in North America.

large, well-educated labor force, reliable and relatively inexpensive electrical power, and proximity to key U.S. markets (less than a day's drive puts Ontario's products within reach of 120 million American consumers).

Assembling cars and light trucks and producing auto parts and accessories is Ontario's most important manufacturing industry. In 2000 Canada produced some 3.2 million cars and light trucks in twenty assembly plants, twelve of which are located in southern Ontario. The auto industry is a major player in Canada's economy but it is the eight-hundred-pound-gorilla in Ontario's, accounting for 12 percent of the nation's manufacturing gross domestic product (the largest segment contributor) but fully 20 percent of Ontario's. The auto industry also directly or indirectly employs one in seven Canadians and an even more dominant one in six people of Ontario.

Mining has also long played an important role in the development of Ontario's economy. Today, the extraction of gold, nickel, copper, uranium, and zinc represents a multibillion-dollar business. In addition to mining, many towns in Ontario have at least one business connected to the forestry industry. The provincial government, which licenses logging

■ The Michigan of Canada

The first large-scale production of autos began in Canada almost a century ago. In 1904, workers at the Walkerville Wagon Works, located in present-day Windsor, put together more than one hundred Model C Fords. The Ford Motor Car Company of Canada soon had numerous competitors, such as Samuel McLaughlin's McLaughlin Motor Car Company (eventually General Motors of Canada) in Oshawa. Following the pattern established in the United States, after World War I the industry slowly consolidated as Ford, General Motors, and Chrysler absorbed the Mercurys and Chevrolets of the auto world.

By 1939, Canada's first four-lane divided highway opened (Queen Elizabeth Way, which runs between Toronto and Niagara Falls). Road building in Ontario was rapid after World War II but the Canadian auto industry struggled in the face of trade restraints. A major breakthrough occurred in 1965 when Canada and the United States signed the Automotive Products Trade Agreement, allowing for increased sale of Canadian-produced cars in the United States.

The "Auto Pact" has had a tremendously beneficial effect on Canada's, and especially Ontario's, economy. Most of the world's largest auto companies now have assembly plants in Ontario, including General Motors, DaimlerChrysler, Ford, and Honda. Canada is the sixth-largest vehicle producer in the world and Ontario plants are the most efficient in North America. The auto industry is Canada's top export industry, accounting for much of Canada's trade surplus of approximately $30 billion in 2000.

Today, Ontario companies account for approximately nine out of every ten cars produced in Canada, and the province exports more cars and trucks to the United States than Japan or any other country. Ontario is also the second leading auto-producing jurisdiction in North America, behind only Michigan.

■ *A woman works on an assembly line at Ford Motor's St. Thomas, Ontario, plant.*

rights, owns 91 percent of the forestland. The forest industry accounts for about 6 percent of Ontario's total exports.

Tourism is the province's third-largest industry. Tourists come from all over the world but mainly from America. They enjoy Ontario's natural wonders and cultural attractions, ranging from kayaking on white-water rivers to shopping in sophisticated urban malls. In 1997, tourist expenditures of $14 billion accounted for more than four hundred thousand jobs, directly and indirectly.

It goes without saying that Ontario's diverse economy provides a large job market for its residents, one of the best in the world. The province has experienced a relatively low unemployment rate of 6–8 percent in recent years, somewhat below the country's average. Unemployment rates are highest in the sparsely populated northwest and northeast, where jobs tend to be limited to forestry, mining, and service industries.

Education and Family

Public education in Canada is primarily the responsibility of the provinces, and to a certain extent each provincial system reflects that particular region's history and culture. In Ontario, all permanent residents between the ages of six and sixteen must attend school. Most students attend publicly funded elementary and secondary schools that are run by district school boards, the oldest form of publicly elected government in the province. Like other provinces, Ontario provides partial funding to Catholic and other independent schools. Ontario also has eighteen universities and twenty-five colleges of applied arts and technology, with more than one hundred campuses across the province. Most of Ontario's 2 million elementary and secondary school students study in English. About one hundred thousand students study in French.

Family life for people in Ontario has changed considerably since the days of the first Loyalist settlers. Although most of its 11.4 million inhabitants still live in a traditional family structure, Ontario's families are on average smaller today than they were even a century ago. A 1996 census recorded approximately 2.9 million families, and 1.9 million of those had children living at home. The average family's size was just 3.1 persons. Although single-parent families were on the rise, they made up only 14 percent of the total families in Ontario.

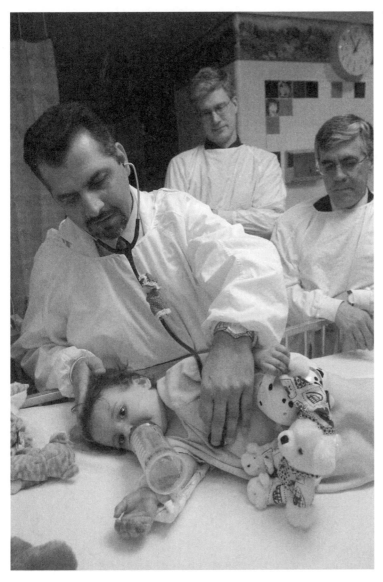

■ *An infant receives top medical attention from a team of doctors after wandering outside and spending the night in the snow. Ontario provides health care second to none in Canada.*

Top-Notch Health Care

Ontario has one of the best health care systems in Canada, and indeed the world. Good health care not only contributes in many ways to Ontario's stable economy, but it also significantly improves the quality of life for its citizens. The quality of care is high, and much of it is available free or at low cost. The Canadian government currently pays seventy-five cents of every health care dollar, compared with the U.S.'s forty-three cents (such payments account in part for the higher overall tax rate in Canada compared to the United States).

Ontario has 36 percent of all hospital beds in Canada (over 128,000 in 1996). The easy availability of good health care shows up in the fact that Ontario had the lowest rate of production days lost per worker in Canada in 2000, and that Ontario enjoys Canada's second-highest total life expectancy at birth rate (78.6 years, behind only British Columbia). The health care and social services industries employed more than 450,000 Ontario residents in 2001, and they were among the highest-paid health care employees in Canada.

Putting Leisure Time to Good Use

Although Ontario's early inhabitants had plenty of leisure time in winter, today's inhabitants have more leisure time year-round. The majority of the people in Ontario today have nine-to-five jobs working for manufacturing or service industries. The average person works just thirty-two hours per week—a little more if they work in factories or other manufacturing jobs, a little less if they work in the service industries, where 73 percent of Ontario's people are employed. What this means is that the people of Ontario have plenty of time—and interest—to devote to a wide range of activities, from creating art to playing sports.

Arts and Culture

For Ontario's native tribes and early pioneers, arts and culture centered on the great outdoors. Over the past century, as life in the province has changed from a rural and agricultural existence to a mostly urban one, the cultural scene has expanded to include the type of music, drama, and other arts found in the sophisticated capitals of Europe. When they are not working or sleeping, the people of Ontario can often be found out and about, perhaps playing or watching a sport, going to a theater for a musical or drama performance, or eating out at any of the multitude of restaurants scattered throughout the province. During the warm summer months, Ontario's many towns and cities offer cultural festivals of all types, where people can enjoy everything from tulips to modern jazz. And during the long, cold winters, there is plenty of time to be creative or engage in winter sports.

The Spell of Winter

When most people think of Canada, they think of winter. And winter without a doubt is an unavoidable element of life in Ontario, affecting cultural and leisure time. But that does not mean the people of Ontario dislike winter, or that it hampers their style. "Winter in Canada is the season of general amusement," noted the eighteenth-century commentator Isaac Weld. "The clear, frosty weather, once snow commences, then all thoughts about business are laid aside, and everyone devotes himself to pleasure. The inhabitants meet in convivial

■ *Crowds of ice skaters take advantage of a beautiful winter's day to enjoy the frozen surface of Ottawa's Rideau Canal.*

parties at each other's houses and pass the day with music, dancing, card playing, and every social entertainment that can beguile the time."[12]

These days, people in Canada still enjoy all those winter activities, and many more. Colorful decorations and millions of lights add a spectacular dimension to many downtown areas. Most notable are the displays on Parliament Hill and along Confederation Boulevard in Ottawa. The boulevard, which unites the banks of the Ottawa River, is lit up and transformed into a romantic place ideal for winter walks.

Cities across Ontario hold festivals, such as the Winter Festival of Lights in Niagara and Winterlude in Ottawa, where festivities are centered on the frozen Rideau Canal, the world's longest outdoor skating rink. Speed skating and dog sledding competitions add to the excitement of the cheering crowd during the ten-day extravaganza. The cityscape is decorated with sparkling, elaborate snow and ice sculptures, particularly in Confederation Park, which is renamed "The Crystal Garden" for the festival. In a new winter art form, some of the world's best artists design and invent fantastic shapes and figures from Ontario's abundant snow and ice, carving sculptures of unmatched beauty and detail.

Other winter activities in Ontario include downhill and cross-country skiing, snowboarding, snowmobiling, ice skating, and Canada's national sport of ice hockey. In all these activities, Ontario residents can choose to participate or simply sit back, watch, and enjoy. In short, there is something for everyone and today, no one in Ontario has to be bored during the long winter months.

Enjoying the Great Outdoors

Whether the weather is warm or freezing cold, the people of Ontario can frequently be found outside, enjoying their great outdoors—be it in the middle of town or the middle of the wilderness. Some people seek peace in the solitude found in Ontario's pristine wilderness. Others prefer to spend their time outdoors closer to home. Between the shores of the Hudson Bay to the north, and Point Pelee National Park in the very south, Ontarians can find the perfect natural backdrop for their favorite outdoor activity.

Not surprisingly for a land that's called "sparkling water," water sports are tremendously popular in Ontario. With thousands of pristine lakes and rivers to paddle, swim, whitewater raft, sail, windsurf, and fish in, there's something for everybody to do. The forested north has become an attractive vacation area and every conceivable sport and activity can be and is played out there, from hunting to rock climbing, hiking to spelunking (cave exploring). Many miles of bike trails in Toronto and other cities can be found throughout Ontario. In Ottawa, officials even close off two parkways to auto traffic on Sundays so bicyclists, joggers, skateboarders, and others can use them. The city's Rideau Canal also offers a host of recreational opportunities: "[U]se the picturesque canal

■ Stunts over Niagara Falls

Most visitors to spectacular Niagara Falls are content to gaze upon the ceaseless, thundering flow of water. Ever since it has been a major tourist site, if not before, a few bold individuals have also seen the Falls as a site for potential adventure. This "x-games" mentality was apparently alive and well during the last half of the nineteenth century, when stunting at Niagara Falls first became a fad.

This era's single most famous performer was Charles Blondin, a French trapeze artist, whom P.T. Barnum sponsored to come to America to be the first to tightrope walk across the river at the Falls. Seating was built for the occasion, and thousands of people paid twenty-five cents each to line the banks of the American and Canadian sides on June 30, 1859. Blondin crossed the rope and deliberately swayed on it as he edged from the American side toward the middle. There he stopped and lowered a line to the *Maid of the Mist* boat waiting below, drawing up a bottle of wine and casually drinking from it before completing his walk.

Just before he reached the Canadian bank, he dumbfounded the mesmerized crowd by doing a backward somersault on the rope. He was given a champagne reception and then announced his intention to return the same way he had come. He skipped and danced his way across the river and into fame and wealth. He spent the rest of the summer doing more routines, crossing the rope on a bicycle, blindfolded, pushing a wheelbarrow, with his feet and hands manacled, and on stilts. Once, he pushed a small stove to the center of the rope, cooked an omelet on it, and lowered it to the passengers on the *Maid of the Mist* below. Another time, more than one hundred thou-

all summer, when you can stroll—or bike or jog—along pathways through landscaped gardens hugging its northernmost stretch through downtown Ottawa."[13]

Outdoor concerts, craft markets, exhibitions, and parades are regular occurrences in towns across Ontario. The multicultural heritage of Ontario's population is reflected in the diversity of these events. Some of them include festivities that celebrate nature and the outdoors, such as the Canadian National Exhibition (the oldest and largest country fair in the world) and the Canadian Tulip Festival, both held annually in Ottawa. The Tulip Festival is the largest of its kind in the world: Millions of flowers herald the spring season and dazzle the eye with colorful floral displays all over the city. The original bulbs were given to the people of Canada by the government of the Netherlands to express its gratitude for the sand people watched Blondin cross the river with his terrified manager on his back—the two nearly fell as the rope swayed under their weight.

Other tightrope walkers followed in Blondin's footsteps, but none could surpass him. For those who wanted fame and fortune but could not walk a tightrope, there was always going over the falls. Fifteen people have gone over the falls in barrels and various other contraptions since the first successful attempt, made by sixty-three-year-old Michigan schoolteacher Annie Taylor in 1901. She survived in an oak barrel fitted with a special harness. Five other daredevils over the past century, however, paid for their attempts with their lives. Today, such stunts are illegal, although that did not prevent a kayaker from going over Niagara in 1990 and a man riding a personal watercraft in 1995. Both died.

■ *French acrobat Charles Blondin (shown here crossing Niagara Falls on a tightrope in 1859) was the first of a line of Niagara Falls thrill seekers.*

protection afforded the Dutch royal family by Canada during World War II.

Ninety minutes outside Toronto lies Niagara Falls, one of the most famous tourist attractions and natural wonders of the world—more camera film is sold here than anywhere else on the planet. The first guidebook, circa 1829, estimated fifty thousand "fashionable, opulent and learned" people visited Niagara Falls yearly. Those numbers exploded in the 1850s as railroads connected urban areas in the United States and Canada with the Falls. Today, Niagara Falls attracts more than 20 million visitors each year, many of them from Ontario.

Hockey and Other Sports

Nothing unites the people of Ontario more than sports, which millions of residents participate regularly in at some

■ *Members of the Toronto Maple Leafs celebrate a 4-3 victory over the Ottawa Senators in game 6 of the 2002 Eastern Conference semifinals. Ice hockey is one of the most popular sports in Ontario.*

level. Surveys suggest that three in five people of Ontario spend at least a quarter of their leisure time engaged in physical exercise or games. Many others coach, officiate, or administrate sport activities.

The most popular sport in Ontario is probably ice hockey, which has long been Canadians' favorite spectator sport. It remains widely played by young and old alike, and in recent years the number of females playing it in Ontario has increased dramatically. More than 520,000 were registered with the Canadian Hockey Association for the 2000–2001 season, and 43 percent of those players came from Ontario. Many more play on streets, lakes, and outdoor rinks and dream of trying out for one of the province's two National Hockey League teams, the Toronto Maple Leafs and the Ottawa Senators.

In terms of spectator appeal, however, professional baseball ranks with hockey at the top of the list. Toronto's Major League

■ Ontario's Famous Athletes

Many people associate Wayne Gretzky, widely acclaimed as the greatest ice hockey player of all time, with the province of Alberta. After all, it was the Edmonton Oilers that Gretzky led to four Stanley Cups in the 1980s. Gretzky also played in Los Angeles and New York before he retired with a host of lifetime scoring records. "The Great One," as he is known by hockey fans, actually was born in Brantford, Ontario, and honed his skills in many of Ontario's numerous ice rinks.

Ontario has yielded numerous other athletes over the years, many of whom rivaled Gretzky as role models if not athletic dominance. One of the province's earliest athletic stars was Toronto's Ned Hanlan, a world-champion rower in the 1870s and 1880s who in his career won an astounding 294 out of 300 races. Hanlan was the first athlete from Canada to win a world championship and gain worldwide recognition. In the decade before the start of World War I, Tom Longboat, who was born on the Six Nations Reserve at Oshweken, set a number of long-distance running records. In 1907 Longboat won the Boston Marathon. Swimming star Alex Baumann, born in Sudbury, won two gold medals and set new records for the 200-meter and 400-meter individual swimming medleys in the 1984 Olympic Games. Elvis Stojko, Olympic silver medalist in the Nagano winter games of 1998, is from Richmond Hill, Ontario. His special talent as a figure skater is a quad-triple combination jump; he was the first to perform this jump during competition.

Ontario has also raised some world-class female athletes. Ottawa-born Barbara Scott won the gold medal for figure skating at the Olympic Games in 1948 and Marilyn Bell became the first person to swim across Lake Ontario in 1954, at the age of sixteen.

Finally, Ontario is the birthplace of the inventor of basketball. Physician and educator James Naismith was born in 1861 in Almonte near Ottawa. Naismith spent his youth in Almonte but was an instructor at a school in Springfield, Massachusetts, in 1891 when he invented basketball by nailing two peach baskets to a gym balcony.

Baseball team, the Blue Jays, attracted more than 4 million spectators, almost double the league average, for three consecutive years during the early 1990s. Attendance has fallen off somewhat since then, as the team has enjoyed less on-the-field success, but some 2 million fans still come to the Jays' home games every year. Operating since 1989 out of a magnificent, retractable-roofed stadium known as the SkyDome, the Blue Jays became the first foreign team to win the World Series in

1992, a feat they repeated in 1993. Baseball and softball are also popular recreational sports in Ontario, with countless local teams and leagues in operation in the summer and autumn.

Then there is football. While Canadian football is similar to American football, it is played on a larger field with twelve instead of the usual eleven players. In Ontario, the cities of Hamilton, Ottawa, and Toronto all boast Canadian Football League teams that compete for the annual Grey Cup championship.

Many other sports are popular as well, especially among younger people. These include swimming, downhill and cross-country skiing, soccer, tennis, bicycling, and windsurfing. More than 650,000 people in Canada play basketball. The Toronto Raptors joined the National Basketball Association in 1996.

In general, people in Ontario take sports very seriously and are proud of the world-class athletes, such as hockey superstar Wayne Gretzky, their province has produced in the past. Both the federal and provincial governments support the network of National Sports Centers, which in Ontario is based in Toronto. The network's goal is to help create an enhanced training environment for high performance athletes and coaches in Ontario—people who are striving for top performance in international competition. In this way, Ontarians help create the future of "Team Canada."

The Arts

Ontario boasts a thriving artistic and cultural scene, stimulated by its multicultural background and financially supported by both the federal and provincial governments. For example, the Ontario Arts Council, which falls under the provincial Ministry of Tourism, Culture and Recreation, funds numerous arts and cultural programs.

Canadian cultural development in general has benefited from the growing diversity of Canadian society. This is especially evident in Ontario. By the 1980s the Anglo-dominated establishment was making room for the diverse cultural groups of Ontario. Most people in Ontario today are more than happy with the multiple channels of American and Canadian radio and television programming that are available to them, including Spanish-, Russian-, and Asian-language programs.

People who prefer their drama and entertainment live can attend any of the numerous theaters that dot the province.

■ Shania Twain

Country singer Shania Twain may seem most at home to her fans when she is singing at Nashville's Grand Ol' Opry, but in fact Twain hails from much farther north. She was born Eileen Regina Edwards in Windsor and raised in Timmins, some five hundred miles (eight hundred kilometers) north of Toronto. The second-oldest of five siblings, her stepfather was a native Ojibwa. Eileen started singing as a youngster, belting out "Country Roads" at her first performance—first-grade show-and-tell. As a youngster she also spent summers working in the Canadian bush with her father on reforestation crews, where she learned to handle an ax and a chainsaw.

Upon the death of her parents in an automobile crash when Eileen was twenty-one, she took responsibility for her three younger siblings and found a job at Ontario's Deerhurst Resort. There she honed her skills singing and acting in musical comedies. In 1990, with her siblings on their own, she took on the Ojibwa name of Shania (shu-NYE-uh)—meaning "I'm on my own"—Twain (her stepfather's surname) and headed to Nashville.

It was not long before her talent as a singer, her songwriting skills, and her beauty queen looks brought her immense popularity and success. Her numerous awards include a Grammy for Best Country Album, *Billboard* honors as Top Country Album Artist, and Canada's JUNO. "I like to give every song its own personality and attitude and to sing each one in its own style," she has said. Her many fans delight in finding out more about, as she sings, "The Woman in Me."

Toronto, which is known as the Broadway of the North, has become the third-largest (after New York and London) theater center in the English-speaking world. With its Broadway-like blockbuster musicals and theater, Toronto manages to present the best in new Canadian plays and avant-garde productions. The city's venues are superb, from the du Maurier Theatre Centre at Harbourfront, a renovated 1920s icehouse, to the elegance of the Elgin & Winter Garden Theatre Centre. This center, a national historic site, is the last remaining, operating double-decker theater in the world. The gilded, fifteen-hundred-seat Elgin lies below; seven stories above is the world's first "atmospheric" theater, the thousand-seat Winter Garden. It is a Victorian fantasy with a ceiling of real leaves (dipped in glycol preservative), columns disguised as tree trunks, and delicately trellised walls.

Shaw and Shakespeare

Farther south, Niagara-on-the-Lake is a lovely small town
eight miles north of Niagara Falls. "With its upmarket shops
and restaurants," notes a travel guide, "well known George
Bernard Shaw Festival and curbs on development, it acts as
a sort of foil to the hype and flash of Niagara Falls. The surrounding vineyards and history-filled parkland add to its
appeal."[14] The Shaw Festival presents the plays of Shaw, as
well as works by some of his contemporaries, each year from
early May to late September. And then there is Stratford,
which sits on the river Thames and comes alive annually
with the Stratford Festival, a celebration of the works of
Shakespeare. Crowds watch some of the best live theater in
North America. Leading actors and directors from around
the English-speaking world come to recite the immortal
words of the great bard.

Ballet and opera enthusiasts are eager to attend the National Ballet of Canada and the Canadian Opera Company,
both of which are in Toronto. Others make a point to attend the
Toronto International Film Festival, held each September for

ten days and nights. Attendees can see the latest film releases, gawk at Hollywood celebrities, and go to glitzy parties. Ontario is the birthplace of a number of famous actresses spanning the past century, from Mary Pickford to Neve Campbell.

Finally, despite the long winters, or perhaps because of them, people in Ontario have maintained their sense of humor. Ontario seems to produce more than its share of comedians, including not only Mike Myers but also John Candy, Rich Little, Martin Short, and Howie Mandel. Ontario's most famous homegrown comedian, of course, is rubber-faced Jim Carrey, who was born and raised in the Toronto area. In elementary school one teacher gave Carrey a regular "performance time" at the end of the school day if he promised to be quiet during classes. When Carrey was only ten years old, he sent his "resumé" to *The Carol Burnett Show*. At age fifteen he did his first stand-up comedy routine at Yuk Yuk's, a famous Toronto comedy club. Carrey continued performing in clubs all over Canada until age nineteen, when he packed his bags and moved to Los Angeles.

■ Tom Thomson's Vision of Rock, Tree, Sky

Thomas John Thomson was born in Claremont in 1877 and raised on a farm near Leith, which is in the vicinity of Georgian Bay. As a youth he had been passionately in love with the outdoors and spent much time hunting and fishing. His art career began to blossom after becoming an illustrator for a Toronto photo-engraving firm staffed with young talents, a number of whom would later become members of the Group of Seven. Thomson began to develop a powerfully individual style on painting trips he would take with coworkers to Ontario wilderness sites, such as Algonquin Park and the Mississagi Forest Reserve.

Thomson's ability to perfectly capture the wild Canadian landscape soon saw his brightly colored, expansive paintings in national museums. As critic Harold Town noted in an article on Thomson in *The Canadian Encyclopedia*, "The small sketch panels and even the larger canvasses could no longer contain his joy and power and needed a larger format to subsume his vision of rock, tree, and sky. . . . With his instinctive technical command of the medium, fueled by an intense love of the North, Thomson, at the time of his death, had all the elements necessary to become a great painter."

Unusual Buildings

Ontario boasts a variety of unusual buildings and museums that show off the rich history, cultural diversity, and grand ambitions of its people. The Ontario Science Museum, for example, is considered one of the foremost museums of science and technology in the world. It was built at the top *and* bottom of a steep ravine—special escalators whisk visitors to the different levels. The museum has six hundred exhibits, many of which are operated by visitors.

Casa Loma ("house on the hill") is an unusual medieval-style castle perched prominently atop a hill in downtown Toronto. It was built in the early 1900s by a Canadian financier who dreamed of living in a European-style castle. He spent some $3.5 million to create an extravagant ninety-eight-room castle, complete with crenellated towers and turrets, secret passages, elaborate halls, an eight-hundred-foot tunnel to stables, and a stained-glass-domed conservatory. Casa Loma is now owned by the city of Toronto and is one of the city's top tourist attractions.

A Painter's Paradise

When it comes to the visual arts, one fact known to painters in Ontario is that colors are at their purest on bright, cold days, which explains why landscapes feature heavily in art from the province. The first truly Canadian art movement was launched by the formation in 1920 of the Group of Seven, composed of seven mostly Toronto-based Canadian landscape painters who rejected their contemporaries' tame European-style paintings. The Group of Seven was particularly inspired by the work of Tom Thomson, an immensely talented painter who had unfortunately drowned at the age of thirty-nine in Algonquin Park in 1917.

The Group of Seven flourished from 1920 to 1933. The style they developed, with Thomson as inspiration, has come to be viewed as uniquely Canadian, featuring bold yet simple designs that capture a sense of large spaces. Other art movements have since supplanted the Group of Seven as a source of national inspiration, but the paintings by Thomson and the mostly Ontario-based Group of Seven remain highly valued and widely shown, within the province and elsewhere.

British Heritage on View

Unlike Quebec, where the majority of people are of French heritage, the most dominant heritage in Ontario is British. Even though the ethnic background of the people of Ontario is becoming increasingly diverse, and the percentage of inhabitants with British ancestors is falling (it is now less than half the total population), the remnants of British culture are prominently on display in today's Ontario.

Ontario's history may not be as long as Quebec's, but the province traces its roots back several centuries to the early pioneers who settled the land. One place where residents and visitors can relive the past is at Upper Canada Village, a "living museum" located 100 miles (160 kilometers) east of Kingston. This re-creation of an early-nineteenth-century Ontario settlement boasts a church, an inn, a mill, pioneer homes, a blacksmith shop, a sawmill, and even a fort. Canals and corduroy roads connect over forty buildings, which can be viewed on foot, as a passenger on an oxcart, or by sailing

■ *Costumed guards reenact a nineteenth-century military drill at Ontario's Fort Henry.*

along the canals in a bateau. Village staff are dressed in pioneer costumes as they perform the various household and community tasks of the day.

Similarly, Fort Henry in Kingston was once the principal stronghold of Upper Canada, guarding the entrance to Lake Ontario and the St. Lawrence River. It has been converted into an extensive museum that includes guards dressed in nineteenth-century uniforms who perform artillery salutes and complex drills with fifes and drums. Such living museums help to teach new generations about some of Ontario's history and rich cultural heritage.

Toward a Global Village

It was Marshall McLuhan, a University of Toronto professor, who coined the phrase "the global village." He is best remembered for his controversial idea that the predominant medium of an age largely shapes the thought of that age. McLuhan suggested that in the 1960s satellite television and other instantaneous communications had made the world into a global village and within that village, "the medium is the message."

Following McLuhan's concept, Ontarians have come up with their own message: even where the challenges of nature are notable, there is pleasure to be gained from enjoying each other's creativity and company. And when it comes to creativity, the people of Ontario will need all they can generate to deal with the issues that face them going into the twenty-first century.

Facing the Global Challenge

C anada's evolution has been based on a tolerance of diversity, whether expressed regionally, politically, culturally, or socially, and this is certainly true for the province of Ontario. As a Toronto newspaper columnist has noted, "Our goal is not life, liberty, and the pursuit of happiness; it's peace, order, and good government. Our history is a story of people trying to settle things in a nice way."[15] Yet as the people of Ontario face the new millennium, they are also confronted with plenty of internal conflict and challenges, ranging from keeping the economy going and maintaining their high standard of living, to dealing with the tens of thousands of new immigrants that continue to settle in Ontario each year.

Balancing Taxes and Services

How best to finance Ontario's extensive network of public services has been hotly debated over the past decade. Until recently Ontario, much like neighboring Quebec, had a reputation for being a big-government, high-tax province. That began to change in 1995 when voters elected as premier Mike Harris, a blunt-spoken small-business owner from North Bay. Over the next six-plus years, Harris and his Progressive Conservative Party government passed several controversial bills aimed at lowering taxes, reducing the size of the provincial government and balancing its budget, limiting welfare, and increasing private investment in the province.

Government supporters said this so-called "Common Sense Revolution" was responsible for steady growth in the province's economy and for creating hundreds of thousands of new jobs in the late 1990s. The province's economy grew faster than that of other provinces (with the exception of energy-rich Alberta) and its unemployment rate in recent years has been lower than the Canadian average. Ontario's overall tax rate, which in the mid-1990s was second highest (after Quebec) by most measures, plunged under Harris's government. A 2001 comparison of provincial and federal taxes faced by a two-income family of four earning $60,000 showed that taxes in Ontario were the second lowest in the country, behind only Alberta. Despite numerous tax cuts, the provincial budget deficit of approximately $8 billion in 1995 was gradually reduced and a balanced budget was achieved in 2001.

Critics of these government policies said that the result was some people getting very rich while many of those less well-off faced cuts in government services and reduced funding for social welfare, health care, and education. Some of the people of Ontario blamed government funding cuts for a recent tragic water contamination incident. In Walkerton, a

■ *Ontario premier Mike Harris addresses a crowd of well-wishers during his farewell tribute in March 2002.*

town about 100 miles (160 kilometers) west of Toronto, a torrential downpour in May 2000 swept bacteria from cow manure into a shallow town well. Over the next three weeks, hundreds of townspeople grew ill. Seven residents, including a two-year-old child, died from drinking the E. coli–poisoned town water. Harris eventually traveled to the town to offer his sympathy, though he denied that cuts he made in public health programs played any part in the tragedy. In early 2002 Harris was replaced as head of the Progressive Conservatives, and Ontario premier, by Ernie Eves. A political ally of Harris, Eves is expected to attempt to continue the recent tax-cutting, reduced-government policies.

A Province of Immigrants

In recent years Ontario has promoted a policy of ethnic diversity and embraced its multicultural character. In 2001 Canada's immigration policy provided residence visas for more than 250,000 new settlers. Almost 60 percent of these new immigrants, 150,000 people, chose to settle in Ontario, more than triple the rate of the next closest province (British Columbia). For the most part the people of Ontario have come to recognize immigrants as a vital resource. Because Ontario's population is, on average, gradually getting older and its birthrate is declining, immigrants are needed to grow the workforce and bolster the province's economy. Immigrants already account for approximately 70 percent of the yearly net increase in Canada's workforce growth, a figure that is expected to rise in coming years to 100 percent.

Exactly who all these new immigrants should be, however, is a controversial issue in Canada and Ontario. In early 2002 federal immigration minister Elinor Caplan was forced to resign in a hailstorm of protest over her "elitist approach." She had proposed radical changes that would have made it much tougher for anyone without an advanced college degree and English or French fluency to immigrate to Canada. Her replacement, Denis Corderre, said that federal policy should not discriminate against skilled workers who do not have college degrees, noting "I'm the son of a carpenter and believe me, my Dad doesn't have a university degree but he can build a house."[16]

Recently Ontario has begun to negotiate with the Canadian government about acquiring more control over the types and numbers of immigrants admitted into Ontario. Provincial

■ Soup or Salad?

For much of the 1990s, an annual UN survey ranked Canada first among the world's nations for quality of life. Other major international surveys have also provided a high ranking for Canada as a safe, healthy, and stable place to live and work. Not surprisingly, much of the developing world views the opportunity to live in Canada, and especially Ontario, with envy. While the vast majority of the people of Ontario welcome new immigrants, the constant flood of new people does put an additional burden on schools, social services, and other government functions.

Increased immigration has also caused some in Ontario to worry about the increasing fragmentation of the province's population. The tendency in Canada has always been for different ethnic groups to maintain their own cultures, as opposed to the "melting pot" model of cultural absorption in the United States. If American culture is like cream soup where everything looks much the same, Canada's, and Ontario's culture in particular, is like a salad where the lettuce is quite different from the tomatoes. What happens, however, when the salad ingredients become too numerous and conflicting?

Recent surveys suggest that such questions prompt ambivalent responses from the people of Ontario. One survey showed that 73 percent of residents believe that a mixture of different lifestyles and cultures make Ontario a more attractive place to live. But another survey indicated that an almost identical percentage agreed with the statement that "the longstanding image of Canada as a nation of communities, each ethnic and racial group preserving its own identity with the help of government policy, must give way to the U.S. style of cultural absorption."

officials note that eight of the other nine provinces already have some type of immigration agreement with the federal government. (Quebec signed the first, and most comprehensive, such agreement in 1991; only Alberta shares Ontario's lack of provincial input on immigration.) Ontario politicians have complained to federal immigration officials that newcomers to the province should reflect overall labor needs. For example, Ontario has been experiencing a shortage in recent years of doctors, nurses, engineers, and construction workers. Also, automotive industry leaders say they need more experienced machinists, tool- and die-makers, and industrial electricians. Ontario officials are also seeking access to immigrant settlement funds now provided by Ottawa to other provinces.

In the new millennium, Ontario's quest for increased control over immigration will no doubt be affected by related issues such as international trade, homeland security in an age of threatened terrorism, and economic growth. Already culturally diverse, and a place thousands are clamoring to enter, it is likely to remain an immigration hotbed for quite some time.

Ontario's First Nations Rise Again

The treaties Canada signed with Ontario's First Nations in the late nineteenth century were one-sided, forcing native peoples to give up much of their land in return for the right to hunt and fish on remotely located reserves. By the mid–twentieth century, life had deteriorated for most native people. Health care was virtually nonexistent in many areas and poverty was endemic. Traditional cultural practices were discouraged by misguided Canadian policies that placed native children in residential schools away from their families and even, from

the 1960s through the 1980s, forcibly removed thousands of "disadvantaged" native youngsters from their parents in favor of nonnative foster homes.

Only within the past decade have the inequities of such policies begun to sink in for most Canadians. Increasingly today, the trend is toward partnership: Native communities look to other Canadians for assistance in becoming self-governing and economically independent. The right to hunt, trap, and fish on certain ancestral lands is also an important aboriginal issue. The Constitution Act of 1982 recognized and fully affirmed these rights and by the end of 1992, the Canadian government at last agreed that Indians and Inuit have the right to be self-governing.

In Ontario today more than 130 First Nations live on some two hundred reserves. These one hundred thousand people control approximately 2 million acres of land. More than fifty land claims, however, have yet to be resolved. These include claims made by the province's most prominent tribes (Algonquin, Ojibwa) as well as smaller tribes like the Mississauga. Some of the claims go back to lands lost more than two hundred years ago. For example, one Mississauga claim says that the tribe is owed damages for land east of Toronto taken illegally from them by the 1788 Gunshot Treaty.

Teaming Up with the United States

Canadians have long felt a sense of economic insecurity, mostly because they tended to compare their prospects and achievements with those of their more powerful neighbor to the south. While many Canadians admire the dynamism of the United States, its influence can be overwhelming. Whether it is because the United States has twice invaded the area of present-day Canada, or more recently because of the perceived threat of American capital and culture to national independence, Canadians have continuously believed that they need special protection from the United States. Only in the twentieth century, and thanks in large part to Ontario, has Canada begun to compete favorably—and cooperate more fully—in the economic realm with its southern neighbor.

Following enactment of the North American Free Trade Agreement (NAFTA) in January 1994, Ontario found itself more than ever a part of the global economy. The province responded quickly to shifts in the global marketplace. Between

■ Paying the Price of Nuclear Debt

A major political battle has emerged in Ontario over recent attempts to open the province's power market to competition from private companies. After almost a century of dominance by Ontario Hydro, the public power company that generates about 90 percent of the province's electricity, in 1998 the Ontario government passed the Energy Competition Act. The law calls for deregulating the electricity market by breaking Ontario Hydro up into five smaller companies. Thus, the generation of electricity will be separate from transmission and distribution, and the government will act as a broker for independent power companies that want to sell their output to the electricity grid. It is an idea that the free-market economists love but that has run into serious practical problems in two of the largest markets it has been tried in recently (California and Alberta).

A primary impetus for the reform was the massive $38 billion debt the public utility has accumulated over the past thirty years. The debt was incurred when the utility made huge investments in building some twenty nuclear plants in three locations. Operating deficits compounded construction cost overruns. The resulting "nuclear debt" looms as a burden that the people of Ontario will be facing for decades to come.

"Unfortunately for consumers," noted Kimberley Noble in a recent *Maclean's* article, "the one certainty in this whole complex exercise appears to be that the days of cheap power are over. Energy Probe predicts that no matter what the government does now, the province's electricity prices are going to be at least 20 per cent higher in two years. Utility executives go even further: they say that what Ontario residents fork over for electricity will at least double in the next five years—and that the overwhelming issue for the Harris government is how it can possibly avoid taking the blame."

Consumers and businesses alike will be watching closely in the next few years to see whether Ontario can succeed and avoid the brownouts, price spikes, and other problems that have hampered other efforts to reform the electricity business.

■ *Ontario Hydro uses massive propeller-type turbines such as this one to generate electricity.*

1994 and 1999, Ontario's total exports increased by more than 40 percent. While export revenue growth was good, the gains were made predominantly in the U.S. market, which was already Ontario's largest export market. In fact, the United States today trades more with the province of Ontario than it does with the entire nation of Japan.

Ontario accounts for over half of Canada's exports, which exceed 40 percent of Canada's gross domestic product. Profits, jobs, and the Ontario economy as a whole depend to a large extent on the competitive success of its goods and services in the international marketplace, which bring in more than $190 billion annually. These exports account for more than 50 percent of Ontario's economy and support in excess of 1.6 million Ontario jobs. Increases in net exports between 1996 and 2000 were responsible for 20 percent of Ontario's economic growth.

Two serious issues cast a shadow over this sunny picture. One is that since the 1960s Ontario has been overdependent on the American market. As Robert Bothwell notes, "Until 1965 Ontario's largest customer was Quebec—and vice-versa. As sales to the United States increased, the relative importance of exports to the rest of Canada declined."[17] The United States is now the destination for more than 90 percent of Ontario's exports. Second, the province is overdependent on fifty very large firms that generate almost 50 percent of its total exports. In the near future Ontario would like to open up more business with the European Union countries, as well as with the Pacific Rim countries, so that its prosperity is not too closely tied to the fortunes—or political whims—of the United States.

Education for Jobs

Over the past half-century, as sophisticated computers and machines replace workers, Ontario has been experiencing a shift within its economy away from labor-intensive jobs in manufacturing and agriculture. Today the two occupations that employ the greatest number of Ontario residents, accounting for almost one in two jobs, are "sales and service" and "business, finance, and administrative." Among the fastest growing occupations are jobs in natural and applied sciences (which grew by some 30 percent from 1997 to 2001); art, culture, recreation, and sport; and social science, education, and government service. The occupations that

grew more slowly over the same period include managerial; health; processing, manufacturing, and utilities; and trades, transport, and equipment operators. Only a small percentage of Ontario workers are now employed in farming or forestry.

■ A saleswoman helps a customer find accessories to match her new outfit. Sales and service positions account for a large percentage of Ontario's total workforce.

In this high-tech, knowledge-intensive labor market, educating Ontario's young people to cope with the new economy is of vital importance to the province. By the mid-1990s, jobs that needed only a high school education or less were rapidly disappearing from Ontario's job markets. On the other hand, in 1997, over two-thirds of the increase in employment was in occupations that needed a post-secondary degree or diploma. It is clear that the workforce of the future has to be better educated if Ontario is to succeed in the highly demanding global economy. Educators in Ontario are increasingly focused on developing an educational system to meet the demands of the new global economy and to allow Ontario residents to maintain the high standard of living they have become used to.

One step toward that goal taken by the provincial government recently was the establishment of the Education Quality

■ Building for the Future

Despite internal conflicts, the economy of Ontario continues to expand. To keep pace, Ontario's government has been working aggressively with the private sector to develop programs that build for the future. The Ministry of Finance, for example, announced the SuperBuild Initiative in 1999. SuperBuild aimed to prepare Ontario's infrastructure for the demands of the new millennium. Ontario had close to $200 billion worth of infrastructure at the end of the twentieth century, about half of it publicly owned (such as communications, railways, and gas lines) and regulated. As part of the SuperBuild program, the government promised to invest $10 billion in capital infrastructure between 1999–2000 and 2004–2005. Another $10 billion of investment would come from the private sector and other partners. SuperBuild infrastructure priorities included the expansion and renewal of Ontario's transportation, post-secondary education, health care, environmental protection, and technology infrastructure—assets such as roads, hospitals, new technologies, and water systems.

■ *Princess Margaret (right) is given a tour of an Ontario hospital. Hospitals throughout the province will benefit greatly from the recent SuperBuild Initiative.*

and Accountability Office (EQAO). The EQAO performs assessments and reviews of schools and offers its recommendations for system improvement to the general public. According to the EQAO, an international test conducted in 2000 involving thirty-two countries and ten Canadian provinces showed that Canadian students did well overall and that Ontario's results were consistent with the Canadian average. Reading was the principal focus of the test and in that area, Ontario students ranked ahead of every participating country but one. In both science and math, Ontario students' scores were about average for Canada but significantly higher than those of students in the United States and Germany.

Toward a New Identity

Ontario has long been a multicultural society. In prehistoric and colonial times, the diverse native cultures that inhabited the land were not immune to intertribal warfare. Then came the British, French, and other European cultures to complicate the mix and to increase the potential for conflict.

On the other hand, the various cultures have always found reasons to cooperate and collaborate, whether it was the French-English partnerships in the fur trade, the British, Scottish, Germans and others who settled amongst each other

■ *Canadians of various cultures and ethnicities attend a memorial ceremony on the front lawn of Ottawa's Parliament to mourn the victims of the September 11 terrorist attacks on the United States. Ontario is one of the most diverse and cosmopolitan Canadian provinces.*

in the eighteenth and nineteenth centuries, or the multitude of other ethnic groups that have sought a new start in the twentieth century. Indeed the formidable challenges of Ontario's development have often forced people to set aside their differences and to work together to achieve their goals.

Even more so than the other provinces within Canada, it is clear that Ontario is destined to remain a multicultural and cosmopolitan society in which public and private enterprise collaborate to make the most of the abundant natural and human resources. Ontario also seems destined to continue to embody the identity of Canada as a whole:

> To an outsider, Ontario seems the most Canadian province of Canada. If Quebec on the east seceded and British Columbia on the west went its own independent way, Ontario would remain the core of Canada, supported, for all their distrust of eastern industrialists, by the Prairie Provinces, and struggling to maintain some connection with the Maritimes . . . . But there would be nothing strange about the character of the country: it would be staunchly Canadian. Every aspect of Canada that has been discussed so far—its difficult size, hard winters, never-ending struggle against American power, English heritage, and mosaic culture—is markedly evident in Ontario.[18]

The eighteenth century was a century of imperialism during which Ontario was developed as an important part of the Canadian colony. The nineteenth century was a century of nationalism, during which Ontario played a major role in the development of Canada as a nation. The twentieth century was a century of globalism, during which Ontario helped Canada more fully participate in world affairs and even earn international recognition as a defender of democracy, as a peacekeeper and safe haven for oppressed peoples, and as the site of one of the world's leading places to live and work. Whatever the twenty-first century may bring, it is bound to add to the richness of Ontario's history.

Facts About Ontario

Government

- Form: Parliamentary system with federal and provincial levels
- Highest official: Premier, who administers provincial legislation and regulations
- Capital: Toronto
- Entered confederation: July 1, 1867 (one of the original four provinces)
- Provincial flag: Red background, Union Jack in top left, provincial shield on the right
- Motto: "Loyal it began, loyal it remains"

Land

- Area: 415,597 square miles (1,076,395 square kilometers); 11% of total land of Canada; second-largest province; rivers and lakes cover 17% of Ontario's territory
- Boundaries: Bounded on the north by Hudson Bay and James Bay, on the west by Manitoba, on the south by the Great Lakes and the states of Minnesota, Michigan, and New York, and on the east by Quebec
- Bordering bodies of water: St. Lawrence River, Lake Ontario, Lake Erie, Lake Huron and its Georgian Bay, Lake Superior, Hudson Bay and its James Bay
- National parks: Bruce Peninsula, Pukaskwa, Point Pelee, Georgian Bay Islands, St. Lawrence Islands, Fathom Five

- Provincial parks: More than 265 encompassing approximately 25,000 square miles (65,000 square kilometers); the largest is Algonquin Provincial Park west of Ottawa
- Highest point: Ishpatina Ridge, 2,275 feet (693 meters)
- Largest lake: Lake Superior, 31,699 square miles (82,101 square kilometers), about one-third of which is located within Ontario; and Lake Huron, 22,999 square miles (59,569 square kilometers), of which about half is located in Ontario; the largest lake entirely within the province is Lake Nipigon, 1,872 square miles (4,848 square kilometers)
- Other major lakes: Ontario, Erie, Lake of the Woods, Simcoe, Nipissing
- Longest river: Albany, 560 miles (900 kilometers)
- Other major rivers: Ottawa, St. Lawrence, Grand, Moose, Severn, Winisk
- Largest freshwater island: Manitoulin, 1,068 square miles (2,766 square kilometers); largest in world
- Time zones: Eastern Standard Time and Central Standard Time
- Geographical extremes: 41°40' N to 56°50' N latitude; 74°21' W to 95°09' W longitude

Climate

- Coldest day: −49° F (−45° C) in Algonquin Park on Dec. 29, 1933
- Greatest five-day snowfall: 78 inches (198 cm) on Dec. 4–8, 1978 in Nolalu, west of Thunder Bay
- Sunniest location: Thunder Bay, average of 2,200 hours of bright sunshine annually

People

- Population: 11,410,046 (2001 census); highest population of provinces and territories; 38% of Canada's total population of 30,007,094
- Annual growth rate: 6.1% from 1996 to 2001 (third-highest growth rate among provinces and territories)
- Density: 27.5 persons per square mile, compared to Canadian national average of 7.8 (10.6 and 3.0 persons per square kilometer)

- Location: 83.3% urban; 16.7% rural; almost 90% live on approximately 10% of land in Ontario's southernmost regions
- Predominant heritages: British, French, aboriginal
- Largest ethnic groups: German, Italian, Dutch, Chinese, Polish, East Indian, Caribbean, Ukrainian, Portuguese, Scandinavian
- Major religious groups: Catholic, Protestant, Jewish, Muslim, Hindu
- Primary languages (first learned and still understood): 72% English, 5% French, and 23% other languages, led by Chinese, Italian, German
- Largest metropolitan areas: Toronto, population 4,682,897, an increase of 9.8% between 1996 and 2001; largest metropolitan area in Canada (one-third of Canada's population is located within a 100-mile/160-kilometer radius of Toronto); Ottawa-Hull, 1,063,664, fourth largest; Hamilton, 662,401, ninth largest; London, 432,451, tenth largest
- Other major cities: Kitchener, Oshawa, Windsor, Sudbury, Kingston, Sault Sainte Marie, Thunder Bay, Saint Catharines
- Life expectancy at birth, 3-year average 1995–1997: Men 75.9 years; women 81.3; total both sexes 78.6, second among provinces and territories (Canadian average: men 75.4; women 81.2)
- Infant mortality rate, 1996: 5.7 per 1,000 live births, ranking sixth among provinces and territories
- Immigration 7/1/2000–6/30/2001:149,868, 59.5% of Canadian total of 252,088; highest of provinces and territories
- Births 7/1/2000–6/30/2001: 130,672
- Deaths 7/1/2000–6/30/2001: 87,565
- Marriages in 1998: 64,536
- Divorces in 1998: 25,149

Plants and Animals

- Provincial bird: Common loon
- Provincial flower: White trillium
- Provincial tree: Eastern white pine

- Endangered, threatened, or vulnerable species: 147, including bald eagle, peregrine falcon, aurora trout, eastern cougar, Lake Erie water snake, piping plover, American badger, Karner blue butterfly, cucumber tree, American ginseng, blue racer

Holidays

- National: January 1 (New Year's Day); Good Friday; Easter; Easter Monday; Monday preceding May 25 (Victoria or Dollard Day); July 1 or, if this date falls on a Sunday, July 2 (Canada's birthday); 1st Monday of September (Labour Day); 2nd Monday of October (Thanksgiving); November 11 (Remembrance Day); December 25 (Christmas); December 26 (Boxing Day)
- Provincial: 1st Monday in August (Simcoe Day)

Economy

- Gross domestic product per capita: $32,373 in 1999, fourth among provinces and territories and 95.7% compared to U.S. average[19]
- Gross provincial product: $426.6 billion at market prices in 2000, first among the provinces and territories and 42.2% of gross national product
- Major exports: Automotive vehicles, parts, and accessories; machines, electrical, metals, pulp and paper, furniture and fixtures, wood-fabricated materials
- Agriculture: Vegetables, fruit, dairy; Ontario is Canada's main agricultural producer
- Tourism: Cultural and recreational attractions year-round; fishing and other water sports; tourism is the province's third largest industry
- Logging: Pulp, paper, lumber
- Manufacturing: Automobiles, motor vehicles of all types, parts and accessories, machinery and equipment, industrial goods
- Mining: Gold, nickel, copper, uranium, zinc

Notes

Introduction: Land of People and Water

1. Quoted in Andrew H. Malcolm, *The Canadians*. New York: St. Martin's Press, 1992, p. 60.

Chapter 1: From Tundra to Toronto

2. Jay and Audrey Walz, *Portrait of Canada*. New York: American Heritage Press, 1970, p. 225.

3. *Environment Canada*, The Canada Country Study: Climate Impacts and Adaptation, "Ontario Region Executive Summary." www.on.ec.gc.ca.

Chapter 2: The Natives and the Fur Traders

4. Lee Sultzman, "Algonkin History," *First Nations Histories*, April 12, 1999. www.tolatsga.org.

5. Quoted in John Carrigg, "Francis Parkman and the Jesuits of North America, Part II," *Eternal Word Television Network*. www.ewtn.com.

6. Robert Bothwell, *A Traveller's History of Canada*. New York: Interlink Books, 2002, p. 18.

Chapter 3: A Loyalist Stronghold

7. Mark Lightbody, Thomas Huhti, and Ryan Ver Berkmoes, *Canada*. Hawthorn, Australia: Lonely Planet, 1999, p. 147.

8. Audrey F. Kirk and Robert F. Kirk, "The United Empire Loyalists?" *Mysteries of Canada*. www.mysteriesofcanada.com.

9. Quoted in Bothwell, *A Traveller's History of Canada*, p. 47.

Chapter 4: Life in Ontario Today

10. Quoted in Donald Carroll, *The Insider's Guide to Eastern Canada*. Edison, NJ: Hunter Publishing, 1993, p. 169.

11. Richard Conniff, "Toronto," *National Geographic*, June 1996, p. 126.

Chapter 5: Arts and Culture

12. Quoted in Edgar A. Collard, *Montreal: The Days That Are No More*. Toronto: Doubleday Canada, 1976, p. 200.

13. Reader's Digest, *Canada Coast to Coast*. Montreal: The Reader's Digest Association (Canada), 1998, p. 135.

14. Lightbody, Huhti, and Ver Berkmoes, *Canada*, p. 198.

Chapter 6: Facing the Global Challenge

15. Quoted in Conniff, "Toronto," p. 134.

16. Quoted in Allan Thompson, "Minister Set to Soften Immigration Proposal," *Toronto Star*, January 30, 2002.

17. Bothwell, *A Traveller's History of Canada*, p. 142.

18. Walz, *Portrait of Canada*, p. 220.

Facts About Ontario

19. *Demographia*, "Canada: Regional Gross Domestic Product Data: 1999." www.demographia.com.

Chronology

ca. 5000 B.C. Distinctive forms of northern and southern Indian cultures emerge in Ontario lands.

ca. 1000 B.C. Pottery is introduced into Ontario from tribes living in lands to the south.

A.D. 500 Iroquois tribes adopt the cultivation of corn.

1300–1400 Iroquois begin to cultivate beans, squash, pumpkins, and sunflowers.

1500–1600 While Algonquin tribes remain hunters, Iroquois tribes live in palisaded farming villages; Iroquois Five Nation confederacy takes shape as a "league of peace."

1534 Jacques Cartier sails the first French ship into the St. Lawrence River.

1613 Samuel de Champlain first visits the Ontario region.

1615 Guided by the Algonquin, French fur traders first travel to Georgian Bay; Champlain penetrates Ontario, reaching to Lake Huron.

Early 1620s French explorer Etienne Brule travels to Lake Superior.

1639 French Jesuit priests establish the Mission of Saint Marie near the village of Ossossane, located near present-day Midland, Ontario.

1659 French fur traders Pierre-Esprit Radisson and Médard Chouart des Groseilliers travel deep into the area of Lake Superior and Lake Michigan.

1670 King Charles II of England grants the Hudson's Bay Company a charter to trade in fur throughout all territories surrounding Hudson Bay, including much of present-day northern Ontario.

1673 Fort Frontenac built at Cataraqui (Kingston) by French; Moose Factory is founded by the Hudson's Bay Company as a fur-trading outpost.

1678 French outpost established at Niagara.

1680–1681 Robert Cavellier de La Salle sails past what is later to become Toronto on his way to the Gulf of Mexico.

1713 The Treaty of Utrecht ends the war between France and England in Europe and North America; all the trading posts, forts, and lands the French had taken from the Hudson's Bay Company during the war are returned to the British.

1720 Small French fur-trading outpost built at present-day Toronto.

1740s French fur posts extended past Ontario, into the prairies.

1763 Treaty of Paris ends the Seven Years' War between England and France and forces the French to give up the majority of its North American territory.

1775–1783 During the American War of Independence, Canada sides with Britain and thousands of Loyalist refugees settle in present-day Ontario.

1791 In response to the tremendous influx of Loyalist refugees after the American Revolution, Britain's Constitutional Act divides Quebec into two provinces: Upper Canada (present-day Ontario) and Lower Canada (present-day Quebec).

1792 Lieutenant Governor John Graves Simcoe arrives in Upper Canada and issues a proclamation offering two-hundred acre lots of land to new settlers.

1793   The town of York (later Toronto) is founded.

1801   German-speaking Mennonites begin settling in the Grand River Valley.

1812   War breaks out between America and England, forcing British and Canadian troops to battle American invaders.

1813   On April 27, the Americans attack and capture York, Upper Canada's capital; they withdraw eleven days later.

1814   Treaty of Ghent ends the war, formalizing the boundary between British North America and the United States.

1816   First steamboat sets sail on Lake Ontario; an act is passed to establish elementary schools in Upper Canada.

1821   Northwest Company merged into Hudson's Bay Company.

1825   Erie Canal completed; waves of English, Irish, and Scottish immigrants, lured by the promise of free land, move into southern Ontario.

1827   Ontario's first university, the University of Toronto, is established.

1837   Uprisings in Upper and Lower Canada over misgovernment by British elites are crushed, but Britain sends Lord Durham to find the cause of the discontent.

1839   The Durham Report recommends reuniting Upper and Lower Canada and increasing autonomy for the colonies.

1840   Union Act unites Upper and Lower Canada to form the Province of Canada, with Kingston as the capital, though Upper Canada is termed Canada West and Lower Canada termed Canada East.

1849   Following antigovernment riots and civil unrest in Montreal, Canada's capital is moved to Toronto.

1855   Bytown is renamed Ottawa; on Christmas Day that same year, members of the Royal Canadian Rifles in Kingston strap blades to their boots, take an old lacrosse ball and some field hockey sticks, and play what is believed to be the first hockey game on ice.

1856   Grand Trunk Railway opened, linking Montreal to Toronto.

1857   North America's first commercial oil well sunk at present-day Oil Springs, Ontario.

1858   Ottawa approved as permanent capital of Canada.

1867   The British North America Act establishes the Dominion of Canada, with Ontario one of four original provinces and the new national capital located in Ottawa.

1870   Rupert's Land purchased from the Hudson's Bay Company by the Canadian government, increasing official size of Ontario.

1876   Alexander Graham Bell invents the first telephone in Brantford, Ontario, and establishes the Bell Telephone Company.

1885   Canadian Pacific Railway completed; copper and nickel deposits discovered along the route bring about the development of Sudbury.

1917   Women are given provincial vote; with much dissent in Ontario the federal government institutes the draft to send more soldiers to fight in the Great War.

1939–1945   Manufacturing almost doubles as Canadian factories, many of them located in Ontario, expand and retool for war.

1976   The CN Tower in Toronto, the tallest freestanding structure in the world, is completed.

1989   The SkyDome opens in Toronto.

2000   Ontario auto industry sets new record, producing more than 3 million cars.

For Further Reading

Books

Craig Brown, ed., *The Illustrated History of Canada*. Toronto: Key Porter Books, 1997. Seven historians take the reader through Canadian history from 1534 to the 1980s, presenting facts, tidbits about everyday life, and the bigger picture in an easy read.

Hugh Durnford, ed., *Heritage of Canada*. Montreal: The Reader's Digest Association (Canada), 1978. A fascinating account of Canadian history with many stories and pictures.

Editors of Time-Life Books, *Canada*. Alexandria, VA: Time-Life Books, 1988. A pictorial essay of people in modern Canada.

Editors of Time-Life Books, *The Canadians*. Alexandria, VA: Time-Life Books, 1977. The book focuses on the opening up of the Canadian west.

Linda Ferguson, *Canada*. New York: Charles Scribner's Sons, 1979. A good basic book for American students interested in reading about the history, geography, and people of Canada.

John F. Grabowski, *Canada*. San Diego: Lucent Books, 1998. An informative and readable introduction to the country as part of the publisher's Modern Nations of the World series.

William Howarth, *Traveling the Trans-Canada*. Washington, DC: National Geographic Society, 1987. A wonderful pictorial essay of life in Canada at the end of the last century.

Works Consulted

Books

Robert Bothwell, *A Traveller's History of Canada*. New York: Interlink Books, 2002. This is a concise and informative history of the country.

Lawrence Burpee, *The Discovery of Canada*. Toronto: Macmillan, 1944. Exciting stories of the earliest Europeans to explore Canada, starting with the Vikings and based on firsthand accounts.

Donald Carroll, *The Insider's Guide to Eastern Canada*. Edison, NJ: Hunter Publishing, 1993. Covers a number of off-the-beaten-track destinations.

Edgar A. Collard, *Montreal: The Days That Are No More*. Toronto: Doubleday Canada, 1976. Offers vignettes and stories about Canada's colorful past.

Mark Lightbody, Thomas Huhti, and Ryan Ver Berkmoes, *Canada*. Hawthorn, Australia: Lonely Planet, 1999. This comprehensive travel guide provides extensive background information on Ontario attractions.

Andrew H. Malcolm, *The Canadians*. New York: St. Martin's Press, 1992. A personal view of Canada and Canadians by the Canadian bureau chief of the *New York Times*.

Kenneth McNaught, *The Penguin History of Canada*. London: Penguin Books, 1988. A short history of Canada written by a professor.

Jan Morris, *O Canada*. New York: HarperCollins, 1990. Penetrating insights from an astute observer of Canada's unique society and culture.

Desmond Morton, *A Short History of Canada*. Toronto: McClelland and Stewart, 1997. An informative and factual history suitable for students.

Peter Newman, *Company of Adventurers*. Toronto: Penguin Books Canada, 1985. Stories about and history of the fur trade that opened up Canada.

Frederick Pratson, *A Guide to Eastern Canada*. Old Saybrook, CT: Globe Pequot Press, 1998. A useful tourist guide.

Reader's Digest, *Canada Coast to Coast*. Montreal: The Reader's Digest Association (Canada), 1998. This book features short descriptions of attractions along Canada's principal highways.

Roger Riendeau, *A Brief History of Canada*. Markham, Ontario: Fitzhenry and Whiteside, 2000. A complete history of Canada to the present day.

John Saywell, *Canada: Pathways to the Present*. Toronto: Stoddard, 1999. A concise account of Canada's history, geography, politics, and economics.

Jay and Audrey Walz, *Portrait of Canada*. New York: American Heritage Press, 1970. A journalistic account of the country's history, geography, and people.

Periodicals

Richard Conniff, "Toronto," *National Geographic*, June 1996.

Kimberley Noble, "Power Crunch," *Maclean's*, April 23, 2001.

Allan Thompson, "Minister Set to Soften Immigration Proposal," *Toronto Star*, January 30, 2002.

Internet Sources

John Carrigg, "Francis Parkman and the Jesuits of North America, Part II," *Eternal Word Television Network*. www.ewtn.com.

Demographia, "Canada: Regional Gross Domestic Product Data: 1999." www.demographia.com.

Environment Canada, The Canada Country Study: Climate Impacts and Adaptation, "Ontario Region Executive Summary." www.on.ec.gc.ca.

Audrey F. Kirk and Robert F. Kirk, "The United Empire Loyalists?" *Mysteries of Canada.* www.mysteriesofcanada.com.

MapleLeafcard.info, Immigration to Canada, "Alberta—Economy & Taxes." www.mapleleafcard.info.

Lee Sultzman, "Algonkin History," *First Nations Histories*, April 12, 1999. www.tolatsga.org.

Websites

Ontario (www.gov.on.ca). Official website of the Ontario government.

Teaching and Learning About Canada (www.canadainfolink. ca). Created for young people, this site provides interesting maps and basic information about Canada, its physical characteristics, and its people.

Index

Picture Credits

About the Author

Steven Ferry writes for U.S. publishers and corporations. He runs a writing business (www.words-images.com) with his wife in Florida.